Good
Mourning

**Finding Hope and Healing After
Losing a Loved One**

By

CHRISTINA HERR

©2024 by Christina Herr

Published by hope*books
2217 Matthews Township Pkwy
Suite D302
Matthews, NC 28105
www.hopebooks.com

hope*books is a division of hope*media

Printed in the United States of America

First paperback edition.
Paperback ISBN: 979-8-89185-075-0
Hardcover ISBN: 979-8-89185-076-7
Ebook ISBN: 979-8-89185-077-4
Library of Congress Number: 2024940765

hope*books
hopebooks.com
*Because the world needs your hope-filled
words now more than ever.*

For Grandpa, who first made me believe
I was a reader and a writer

Table of Contents

PART 3: HOPE

Author's Note

Dear Reader,

I've wanted to write this book for years, but I wish I never had to. I'm so glad it's found its way into your hands, but I wish you never had to read it. That's the thing with grief and loss: they will always come with multiple emotions. Learning how to navigate and hold space for all of them is tricky but necessary.

Throughout this book, we will dive into my losses—the losses and goodbyes that saddened me, shook me, and ultimately shaped me. We will catch glimpses of eight-year-old me after Mom woke me up early in the morning to tell me Dad had died after another heart attack. We will revisit the losses and lessons learned from my beloved grandparents who taught me and molded me and helped Mom when she was too mentally unstable to care for herself, let alone me—all of whom I lost when I was between the formative ages of 17 and 22. We will travel to my late twenties, finding out that one of my best friends was suddenly just... gone. She was taken too soon by a drunk driver. We will also explore the loss I experienced in my early thirties when, just after I finally felt like I understood my mother and had greater empathy for all she went through, just when our relationship was closer than I ever thought it could be, I cared for her during her last months of life as colon cancer fought against her body and ultimately won. It's not easy to go back and relive all of those losses, just as I'm sure it may have been a bit much to list them all here, so matter-of-fact. But are we ever really ready for the impact of loss? No matter how "prepared" we may think we are, it always feels like a punch to the gut.

Chances are, you are reading this book because you, too, have suffered a loss. Maybe you saw it coming, or maybe it came as a complete shock, but it happened, and here we are. Shaken, but still here. Wondering how to get through the next year, hour, lifetime, second. Yet still, you are here. Feeling like you are in the darkest black of night and that you'll never see the sun again. But, look at that—here you are. If I've learned one thing about the weight of grief, it's that it's too heavy to carry on your own. When we open up about it, speak about it, acknowledge it, and let others share the load, it frees us. When we bottle it up, it's like a whole flock of birds locked in a cage, one that was never designed to hold such a large number of fluttering wings.

Acknowledging grief is akin to opening the door of that cage and letting those birds fly free, allowing them to stretch up above the fog and clouds and remember what it's like to feel the sun. In this book, while you go with me through my own journey of grief, I hope you find some mirrors and similarities that help you feel less alone. Some of your experiences may look a lot like mine, and some may be very different, but they are connected by the common thread of grief. At some points in this book I will touch on elements of my faith in God as they relate to my grief journey, but I do not claim to be a theologian or expert in matters of faith. I want to make it known that no matter your faith background or lack thereof, this book is for you. All are welcome at this table.

Together, we will explore coping mechanisms, celebrate small victories, and pay tender tribute to the imperfect but cherished loved ones we lost along the way. We will also connect through poems I penned at various stages before, during, and after losses, through narratives, and through practical encouragement and advice for you, the reader. Together, we will cherish memories, honor legacies, and find solace in the bonds we share with those who have departed. At the end of each chapter, you will see a *Pause and Reflect* question, which is designed to encourage you to do just that: take a breath, think about the question, and be introspective about what it is asking. These prompts can be for you to think about on your own and write answers or discuss with others. There is no right or wrong way to engage with the questions. They are there to help you in whatever way works best for you.

Because no two grief journeys are exactly the same, I won't promise to have all the answers or be an omniscient grief guru. I do, however, promise to share what I know, to hold space for you and your hurt, to do my best to help you uncage the winged animal known as your grief. I promise to help you feel the sunlight again.

Let's begin.

Love,

Christina

PART 1:

HURT

Seismic

It lies dormant, an earthquake waiting.
A fissure. A crack at the surface
Of the Earth
Until
    Suddenly

I hear her favorite song on the radio
And I don't know what to do with myself.
The crack widens and the
Earth
    Explodes

The seismic shift shakes underneath my feet
Tosses me among the memories
And won't even dare to let
Me
    Breathe

1

The Timeline

Spoiler alert: there is no timeline. You have been through a loss, and it will forever change you. Whether you had time to prepare or it hit you in an instant, this is hard. You will survive this, but it's still hard. Allow yourself to recognize that and feel the emotions you need to feel. Don't worry about timelines or schedules or some magical point at which everything will feel normal again. With grief, there's no such thing as normal, anyway. Some people may seem to heal quickly; some take longer. There is not necessarily a right or a wrong.

I sat across from my friend Holly at my kitchen table about a year after I lost my mother. She had recently suffered the same loss. Our kids ran around the house, grabbing cookies off the counter on their way through the kitchen. We tried to have a conversation amid shrieks and squeals, stopping every so often to tell the kids to settle down or be nice or go outside if they were going to be so loud. Holly looked at me earnestly, veering away from the safer topics of our favorite dinner recipes and the upcoming school field trips we both planned to chaperone.

"Christina, it's now been one month since I lost my mom. How long does this take?"

"How long?" I asked. "You mean, the grief?"

"I guess," she replied. "This sadness. This pit. The whole world feels heavy, and I feel like it will never end. Tell me it does at some point. It has to. Right?"

I told her, with sincerity, that the newfound weighty heaviness does, in fact, end. You will remember it and feel it in different ways, but it will not always feel quite as massive as it does in the early days. I recounted feeling the same way in the immediate aftermath of losing my mom, sometimes feeling like the weight would crush me. But there I was, sitting across from her, still breathing. Remembering how to talk without crying, to laugh without guilt, and to advise without feeling like a fraud. Time doesn't heal everything, but it does help you regain your footing after the giant tumble you take when you lose someone you love.

Maybe you're thinking the same thing as my friend, wondering if this pain will ever go away. It will always be a part of you in some way, but it will not always feel as heavy as it does in the very beginning. In the beginning, it is fresh. In the beginning, it is a deep, gaping, unsightly wound. In the beginning, allow yourself to feel it and sob when you need to. I wish I could tell you there is a set timeline, but we all know that is a lie. I wish I could say you will certainly experience A, which will lead to B, then C, and it will all happen within X number of days. The truth is, there is no perfect linear system tied up neatly with a bow or an equal sign. But I can tell you the world will not be in grayscale forever. Colors will show up again. The weight will start to lift. It may not seem like it today, but trust me. What feels insurmountable right now will someday be a mountain that you will look back on and say, "I climbed that." You'll be like the proud tradesmen—carpenters, electricians, roofers—who pass a building and say to their kids in the backseat, "You see that building? I worked on that building," even if they have passed and proclaimed the same thing a dozen times before. You'll reflect on the memories of this season and be able to say, "You see that grief? I worked on that grief." It may be the hardest thing you ever do, but trust me when I say you *can* do it.

In 2013, I got the worst phone call of my life. My best friend, Amber, called me and immediately told me I should sit down. My first thought was that something terrible had happened to one of her grandparents, with whom she was incredibly close. I knew I would want to be strong for her. I would know what she was going through, and I would not need to sit down. Naively, I kept standing. She quickly told me that one of our closest friends, Angie, had been in a car accident late the night before. She had been driving home from a late-night shift at a local 24/7 grocery superstore when a car headed in the opposite direction hit her car head-on. The driver of the other vehicle was drunk and also carried his four-year-old son.

"She's going to be okay, right?" I asked. Surely, I thought, Angie was banged up, but she'd come out of this. Maybe she would need surgery, but she would be okay.

"Right?!" I pleaded again.

But that wasn't the case. The opposite, in fact. The impact had taken her life instantly. In the months to come, and even now, that was about the only solace we could find—that she didn't suffer. For many weeks after Angie's death, I was in a fog. We traveled back to our home state of Michigan for the funeral. Me, my husband, our four-year-old son, one-and-a-half-year-old son, and six-month-old daughter were in the minivan. I was fueled by adrenaline, shock, and a playlist of music from my teenage years, driving through the night to get to Michigan in time for the funeral. I walked into the funeral home and was greeted by the friends I grew up with, the friends who were all major players in my coming-of-age story. We all wore pairs of Converse All-Stars, Angie's signature footwear, in her honor. Different colors juxtaposed against our black dresses. We held each other, we cried, and we were angry and confused and shocked and hurt—together. The loss of a peer, of a friend as close as a sister, was unlike any loss any of us had ever faced.

Somehow, in little bursts, we were able to laugh about something funny Angie had said way back when. She was the funniest one of all of us, no question. There were so many pictures on the photo boards they had put together. So many memories. It was actually on that trip home that something cracked open within me, reminding me to write again. Angie and I both loved to write. She talked of becoming a novelist or poet and moving to London. I wrote poetry and personal essays, but after high school, I just stopped. On that trip up to Michigan, after the funeral, I was looking through some boxes in my childhood home and found old notebooks, journals, and diaries that I had filled when I was a child and teen. In the busy season of starting a family and a career, I had somehow tucked that part of me away and had almost forgotten all about it. It reawakened the desire to write again. It became a very therapeutic pursuit in the months that followed. Something cracked open and allowed me to remember that I was once "Christina" and not only Mom and Mrs. Herr the teacher. A seed was planted. A whisper was heard. "Write," it said. I would give back every word I've written in the past decade if it would bring Angie back, but since that's just not possible, I find comfort in the words that have been spilling out of me in the years since her passing. I hate that her death happened, but if I can bring any good out of it, if I can pull at the threads and find something beautiful, it's what I need to do. So, word by word, it's what I did in the aftermath.

Before the writing brought me solace, and once we were back in North Carolina where we were living at the time, it was time for me to go back to work. I was a first-grade teacher, and although I loved my job, I really did not know how I was supposed to make it through.

I wanted to scream and cry and yell and tell the world how unfair it all was. I could not understand how people could go about their days smiling as if they were happy, as if joy could exist at a time like this. Being a typically positive person, I really wrestled with these feelings. I wasn't used to them. But these were not typical times. I had to put a smile on my face like a bumper sticker on an old jalopy because I didn't want my students to be burdened by my sadness. I had to pretend in public, but in private, I let myself feel what I needed to feel. I would wash dishes and stare at the soapy sink water, thinking of Angie. I watched the Halloween classic movie *Hocus Pocus* for the first time that year, recalling that it was her favorite. I called and texted two other friends, putting together a scholarship fund at our high school alma mater in Angie's name, all of us trying to find a purpose in the pain. As previously mentioned, I began to write again. It all helped. It didn't erase the hurt all the way, as nothing could, but it helped. Looking back, I'm glad I didn't put pressure on myself to feel "better" or "over" the grief by any specific deadline. The light started to come through eventually. There were certain things that helped me (more on that later). But when you are faced with that question of "How long does this take?" give yourself grace, space, and time. There's no perfect answer. I wish there were. I was the precocious child who actually liked taking tests back in school because I loved determining the correct answer. It felt good to know something with certainty. With grief, it is not two plus two, or which planet is the largest in the galaxy, or what is the difference between fact and opinion. With grief, it is uncertain. Two plus two may equal four, but loss plus that ache in your chest equals something different for all of us. Feel what you need to feel when you need to feel it.

You will make it through, my friend. Not every day will be as hard as the first, and sometimes, there will be days far down the road where you fall apart all over again—but not forever. You also might hear of other people processing their grief on a timeline that looks much different than yours. Resist the urge to judge yourself or them, or to compare your journeys. Theodore Roosevelt once famously said, "Comparison is the thief of joy." Your grief journey does not have to look like someone else's. Don't rush the process, and don't feel bad if you experience the opposite and it takes you a shorter time than most to heal. For today, know that it is okay to let your emotions pour out. Your journey is yours alone and doesn't have to fit into a certain-sized box.

PAUSE AND REFLECT:

Have you felt pressured to "move on" in a specific time frame? Do you feel the pressure is coming from other people or from within?

Fighting for Air

I was a thousand miles away when I got the call.
I didn't believe it at first.
Maybe just send flowers, someone said,
like that would be enough.

Our tires pounded pavement on I-40
Three kids in the backseat,
One with a broken leg
which is another story for a different day.

Eyes bloodshot from exhaustion and salty tears
I changed into a dark gray dress and
Slipped on an old pair of All-Stars.
They always were your favorite.

The photo boards hit me like a wave
Ready to drown me.
Shots of all of us when life was easier
And responsibilities were few.

Those boards, they tried to break us
but they didn't. Not all the way at least.
They reminded us of who we were
and where we came from.

And where you would want us to go next.

2

The Roller Coaster

When I was in junior high, the school sponsored a weeklong field trip for the eighth graders to go to Washington, D.C. We spent time seeing many historical sights, including the Capitol building, the Lincoln Memorial, the Washington Monument, and the Smithsonian Museum. But the part that ended up being the most fun, especially for a group of fourteen-year-olds from a small town, was the day we spent at a big amusement park called Kings Dominion. There were rides of all sizes, food stands, and souvenir shops, and it was such a blast.

My friend Brooke and I were in a group together and decided to ride a huge roller coaster—the first one I had ever ridden in my life. I was so nervous while we were waiting in the line. I remember Brooke and I, being weirdo middle schoolers, clung to each other, pretending to be scared toddlers, and spoke in baby voices, saying, "But mama, I don't wanna ride!" even though we were waiting there of our own free will. My knees were shaky. I wanted to do it, but I was also terrified. We finally got buckled in, and I screamed the whole time. It was unlike anything I had ever experienced, creaking all the way up to the highest peak, whooshing down at top speed, and going upside down so my stomach did somersaults. It was intense, and then, just as soon as it began, it was over, and I was left feeling exhilarated. After all the fear and nervousness, I looked at Brooke, and we both nodded in such a way that we knew meant, "Oh my gosh, that was something. Let's do it again." We experienced so many emotions, including the highest of highs and the lowest of lows, all in such a short period.

Hmm. Sounds familiar, actually. Doesn't it?

In the aftermath of a loss, your emotions will likely be all over the place. You might cry one minute, laugh at something the next, and then feel guilty because you're wondering if you should be laughing during such a sad season in your life (the answer is yes, it's fine, but more about that in a later chapter). In fact, you may experience any or all of the following emotions as a result of or correlation to your recent loss. Of course, this list is not exhaustive, and you may feel other emotions as well, but here is a start:

- Sadness
- Anger
- Guilt
- Anxiety
- Fatigue
- Shock
- Loneliness
- Helplessness
- Relief
- Numbness

A solid four or five years after Angie died, I was listening to Ed Sheeran's hit song "Castle on the Hill" and got hit by a wave of sadness. I told you there were no set timelines! I have loved that song since the first time I ever heard it, and I have always connected to the lyrics. Sheeran's lyrics are basically a love letter to his hometown and his childhood friends. They describe what his various childhood mates are up to now and how all those people had a hand in raising him. It resonated so deeply with me.

It made me think of Angie and Amber and Mary and Brooke and Candice, and all the other friends from our hometown who helped shape my childhood and teenage years. These people raised me. That rural town in Michigan will always feel like home. I wanted to call Angie and tell her about the lyrics. I thought about when Ed Sheeran's first album came out and wondered if she ever had a chance to hear him sing. I was sure she would have loved him. She might have avoided his newer stuff after he hit it big because she always loved underground music more than mainstream. But I was so sad and upset that she would never hear it. I couldn't call her and tell her about "Castle on the Hill." One of his songs would never be found on one of her famous mixed CDs. She would have moved on to playlists on Spotify anyway, but she never even got the chance, and it felt so wrong.

As I listened to those lyrics, I had to let myself name the emotions I was feeling. I had to say, "This sucks and I'm angry! I hate this! I wish she were here!" Just naming your emotions can help you work through them. The alternative is stuffing them down inside, pretending they don't exist, and later erupting like a volcano—because, eventually, it will all come out in some fashion. Naming the emotions as or right after you feel them creates a healthy emotional and psychological response that allows you to feel a sense of greater ease and self-awareness. Don't cover them up or stuff them down.

Maybe if you just lost a loved one, you snapped at your spouse or your child over something trivial. Maybe you stepped on a Lego or found that your child moved your phone charger yet again, and you lost it; yelled, cussed, the whole nine yards. I'm willing to bet that when that happens, it might have little to do with the Lego or the phone charger. It might be a form of emotional displacement, in which you are upset about something else and project that onto whatever or whoever is closest to you. It's not a healthy pattern to develop, and it can be minimized by honoring and naming your emotions as they come up. Maybe you say them out loud—whispered to yourself if you're driving somewhere or working from home in a quiet space. Maybe you write them in a journal, letting the words spill out without worrying about purpose, form, or correctness. Maybe you call someone close to you and let them know how you are feeling. Those heavy emotions are valid and expected and a normal response to grief. What we don't want to do, however, is stay parked in those heavy, negative emotional responses forever. We eventually want to trudge through the muddy waters of grief and let the light back in. But remember, there is no deadline. It won't always feel this heavy. And along the way, you have the power to navigate your big emotions by accepting that they do exist and they do affect you.

When Brooke and I went on that roller coaster back in eighth grade, we knew what we were in for—to an extent. We watched several groups go before us, heard their shrieks, and saw the mixture of terror and elation. We figured we knew what it would be like once it was our turn. But the truth is, we didn't really understand until we went through it ourselves. And even though we were best friends feeling similarly about the whole thing, our experiences were still unique and varied. She loved the loopty-loops the most, while I hated them. I handled the upward ascent a little better, whereas that part terrified her. We experienced different emotions at different points in the ride, even though we were side by side. There are parallels to the grief roller coaster there. You and someone else might be on the same ride, so to speak, but your emotions will rise and fall at different points. Are either of you processing things wrong? No, that is not the case.

Just like Brooke and I each had our own unique experiences on the same ride, grief is a profoundly personal journey. As we navigate the highs and lows that follow a loss, it is important to remember that there is no one-size-fits-all approach to grieving. We each had our own distinct moments of fear and exhilaration on the roller coaster, and so too will each individual experience their own mix of emotions and challenges during their grief journey. These variations do not mean any one person is processing things "wrong," just differently. When we all understand that, we are better equipped to offer grace, empathy, and support to those around us and to ourselves as we ride the roller coaster of grief together.

PAUSE AND REFLECT:

Think of a recent time when you went from a low to a high emotional state or the opposite—high to low. What was the context? What could you try at that moment to ground yourself and bring about greater emotional balance?

Buoy

Gasping for air
Limbs flailing
Can't stay afloat
Water filling my lungs
Am I going to make it?
Am I ever going to breathe
Deep again?

And then
I see a buoy,
thrown by a helper
Reaching out
Giving me something
To clutch
And taking me to the shore
Where I can inhale
And exhale

It saves my life and
Now I know how to do
The same thing for
Somebody else

3

The Shipwreck

One day, right after my mom died, a friend of mine, Beth, homesteader extraordinaire, brought over a roasted chicken (that she cared for, raised, and butchered herself), potatoes and vegetables (from her garden), and these black and white cookies I had never seen or heard of before. Being from the Midwest, I didn't realize they were famous in New York. Beth is an East Coast native, and they had been a big part of her childhood; her grandmother made them whenever anyone in her family needed a pick-me-up. We stood around my kitchen island, and after sharing the reheating instructions, she shared something that made so much sense and continues to stick with me years later. She had heard this story from someone else, who heard it from someone else, and so on, like those old chain letters you might have randomly received in the mail in the 1990s. The only attribution I could find was an anonymous online post from at least a decade ago, so I'll do my best to give the summary justice.

As we have established, grief comes in waves. But to further the analogy, it comes in waves because losing someone is like being involved in a shipwreck. When it first happens, you are drowning at sea, and the flotsam is all around you. Everything you see in the water reminds you of the beauty that once was your glorious vessel, but now it is in shambles, no longer there. All you can do is hopefully find a piece of the wreckage, hold on for dear life, and float. You have to take things one second at a time because you are just trying to stay alive.

At first, the waves around you are so tall, crashing around you and not giving you time to think, speak, or catch a breath. You're still in hold-on-and-float-and-just-survive mode. A few weeks—or maybe months—go by, and you realize the waves are still just as tall but not coming as close together. Sometimes, you even feel like you can breathe or think about your next move. You begin to be able to function. In between the waves, you remember how to live life.

Sometime later, and this is different for each person, you realize that the waves are getting shorter. What used to be an 80-foot wave is now only 70 feet tall, then 60, then 50, and so on. Their frequency continues to decrease. In between, you can catch your breath, shop for groceries, and laugh. But you never know what might trigger another one. It might be a quote, a restaurant, their favorite flower, their most hated Christmas song—anything goes, and a wave crashes over you. But in between them, you are rebuilding your life.

These waves will decrease in size and frequency, but they'll never vanish all the way. Sometimes you'll spot them a mile out, and sometimes they'll crash over you out of nowhere, but whatever the case, you will know that somehow you will survive. You may be waterlogged, and your lungs may feel like they can't quite function, and you may be clinging to a small piece of the wreckage, just grasping for a way to stay afloat, but you know that you will. You'll face waves, and the unfortunate truth is that you'll face whole new shipwrecks as well, which is hard, horrible, and tragic. It's also beautiful, lovely, and precious because what makes the shipwrecks so hard to navigate are the memories and relationships attached—the love.

I have come back to this analogy time and time again. I've found that in the aftermath of loss, analogies give your mind something to relate to, something to provide an anchor point. The shipwreck is a powerful and logical one. Another one I have heard is from Twitter user Lauren Herschel, who used the metaphor of a ball and a box. Imagine a two-dimensional box with a pain button on one side of the box. Also in the box is a large ball, which represents grief itself. When you first go through the loss, the grief feels enormous and fills every inch of your life. It is omnipresent, hard to handle, and most definitely hard to ignore (nor should you). With every move you make, that bouncing ball will inevitably hit the pain button. There's no way to avoid it at first. This is when you are trying to adjust to this new reality, and you may try various coping mechanisms. Maybe you try to keep yourself busy, maybe you isolate, maybe you amp up self-care, or maybe you make zero time for self-care because you are too sad to even think about it. Whatever the case, that bouncing ball keeps hitting the pain button and sounding the alarm bells in your heart and mind.

There will be some days when you feel like the pain is never-ending. The darn ball takes up so much space you wonder if anything else will ever be able to fit around it. You'll wonder if it will always feel so all-consuming. Then, perhaps slowly at first, you realize the ball is getting a little smaller, losing a little bit of air. There is room for other things in your life and in your thoughts. You smile and mean it. You laugh and feel good instead of guilty. You want to be around people without screaming. You have a whole day where you feel like your former self before the grief took over. The ball is getting smaller, but it is still there, bouncing around. Sometimes, it bounces around inside of you and hits that pain button again. There are times when you know it's about to hit the button and other times when it completely catches you off guard. This pain button may be hit the day after the funeral, sure, but it might also be pushed five, ten, or fifteen years down the road. A song plays over the speakers at the grocery store, or you visit a place you haven't visited since you were there last with your person, and just like that—the button is hit, and the pain flares. It may not come as often as it once did, but the pain will never vanish completely. And what's more, it doesn't matter how long it has been; the pain button might still cause the same level of pain as it did when the loss was fresh, and the grief ball was giant. The frequency has changed, but the intensity may very well remain the same when triggered.

The fact that the pain isn't felt as often or perhaps as strongly doesn't mean you don't miss your person anymore. You will always miss them, but you have learned to accept the reality of the loss, and you understand that the metaphorical ball of grief is not meant to loom large forever. Other shapes will take up space in the box, maybe in the form of new or renewed interests, people, professional commitments, etc. These new additives to the box will help reduce the chances of the grief ball bouncing around so much and hitting that pain button. The healing that comes from this process will allow you to better acknowledge and accept the loss itself, while also feeling grateful for the memories you made and the time you shared with your loved one.

Whether you think of these pain triggers as waves out at sea or a bouncing ball hitting a pain button in a box, the conclusion here is that the grief experience is going to look different for all of us. We will all have different waves or different pain points. Hearing Frank Sinatra, seeing anything related to St. Patrick's Day, watching old musicals, flipping through old photo albums—they have all caused waves for me since that was the day

Mom died. Mom's birthday and Mother's Day both cause waves. Driving past the spot where Angie's accident occurred, eating a raspberry, and remembering the countless hours I spent helping Grandpa Conde tend to his fruit and vegetable garden are all waves. Sometimes, I can see them coming from a mile away, and sometimes, they wash over me out of nowhere. The same will likely happen to you. As the years pass, the waves will get smaller, and the pain button will get pushed less and less, but it will never go away altogether. And that's okay, really, because I can't honestly say I'd want it to. Although the waves can be painful, they are reminders of lives lived and love experienced. We accept the hurt while also clinging to the good memories.

PAUSE AND REFLECT:

Considering the shipwreck analogy, what waves of grief might you anticipate over the course of the next year?

Who What When Where Why How

Who will be there to walk me down the aisle?
Your brother will walk you and it will
Be one of his proudest days
Grandpa will be there waiting at the end
In a wheelchair to give you away. Cherish this,
Because he doesn't have much time left.

What will I do without your jokes?
You will still laugh, and when you do,
Think of me. Your kids will be funny, too,
And there will be plenty they say
That you wish you could tell me.
Trust that somehow, someway, I hear them.

How will I know how you really felt?
You'll know it because you feel the same
Way about your own children. You'll know it
Because you have my journals, my shaky handwriting
You'll know it because of our
Complicated but profound connection.

Why, though? Why?
Alas, some questions aren't meant to have an answer.

4

The Questions

After Angie died, I didn't plan a formal eulogy, but I knew I wanted to say something at the funeral. What can you say to sum up over a decade of friendship that ended much too soon and much too suddenly? I wasn't exactly sure. We were all so shocked and broken. None of us were scheduled to give a formal speech, but many of us knew we wanted to say something. Somehow, I mustered the courage to get up there first.

The first thing I did, knowing Angie would approve, was pull out my phone and pull up the YouTube video of the Golden Girls theme song: "Thank You For Being a Friend." I let it play, pausing to share the story of Angie teasing me endlessly once she found out that I originally thought the lyrics were, "You would see the biggest gift would be from me, and the 'heart attack' would say, 'Thank you for being a friend,'" as opposed to the actual and more logical words, "card attached."

Anyway, after the song finished, I started by saying that as a mom of three young children and an elementary school teacher, I am used to answering questions all day long:

Can I have a snack?

How do I tie my shoes?

What is 3+5?

How do I spell [insert any word here]?

Why is the sky blue?

It's one of the major reasons I entered the field of education: I love being able to answer questions, share knowledge and strategies, and see my students or my own children light up with joy when they realize they have learned something new, satisfying their curiosity. Answering questions is a joy—or so I thought. It turns out it's more of a joy if I have the answer, or at least if it can be found somewhere. But as I learned with this situation, this loss, this tragedy, there was no answer for the giant, ugly, terrifying question of "WHY?"

Why did that man have to drink so much that night?

Why did he get behind the wheel?

Why did Angie work that shift?

Why did she take that route home?

Why isn't she here right now, shouting out "surprise!" and giving her signature, purposely oversized smile, revealing the punchline of her only horrible joke?

The questions that follow the loss of a loved one are profound and sometimes paralyzing. As I stood there in front of my fellow mourners, I knew that these questions were not unique to me. In moments of grief, we all grapple with the same fundamental questions. The most persistent and haunting question is, of course, "Why?" It echoes in our minds, an unrelenting refrain that seems impossible to silence. We seek answers, looking for some logical explanation to make sense of the senseless.

Unfortunately, standing at the podium, looking out at everyone who knew and loved Angie, there were no answers to any of those whys. And when we don't have answers, it can be incredibly frustrating and defeating. It can drive you mad if you let it. In the moments, days, months, and even years after losing Angie, it helped to turn to my faith for guidance, even if it didn't provide the concrete answers that I would have loved to elicit.

The answer is that bad things happen to all of us. The answer is that we live in a broken world. The answer is that even though bad things are real and evil is real, we are not alone. God is still for us, even when bad things happen. Our sorrows grieve Him, too. There is a well-known Bible passage in chapter 11 of John where Jesus finds out that a close friend of His, Lazarus, has died. Now Jesus, being the Son of God, knows how the story will end. He knows that when He goes to this friend's bedside, He has the power to bring him back to life—which He indeed does. But in the moment, He feels the sorrow and allows it to show. The shortest verse in the Bible describes His response: "Jesus wept" (John 11:35). He is with us in our sadness and understands what it is like to go through loss, to mourn, and to weep. It is a comfort to remember that we are not alone in this season or any other.

It is normal and natural to ask the "why" questions. If the loss rocks your world and you find yourself angry at a person, at the world, at God—guess what? That is normal, too. It's real. It's hard not to ask those questions and wonder what the heck kind of plan this was all a part of. It may even cause a deconstruction or a hesitancy to consider your faith further. Simply put, it can cause a beautifully built house of cards to come crashing down, leaving you with the not-so-fun game of fifty-two card pick-up.

The questions persist in our minds, but they are not a sign of weakness or a lack of faith. Rather, they are a testament to the complexity of the human experience. It is also a testament to the depth of our love for the person we have lost. We question, we doubt, and we seek understanding, and all of these emotions are valid in the face of such profound loss. As it pertains to faith, you are not alone when you ask those questions, and God can handle all of them. You have heard the phrase, "He wrestled with the idea..." or "She wrestled with God..." or "He wrestled with the thoughts and questions in his mind..." Think about the imagery of wrestling. Does wrestling involve sidestepping an issue or being polite? No, you are all tangled up. When you are wrestling—and I mean in the literal physical sense, as in two high school wrestling athletes—there is constant movement, grit, determination, sweat, and sometimes tears. It is an involved process!

In the end, "wrestling," or considering those questions and working through them, helps you untangle some of the emotions that you are feeling. Wrestling with these questions is an essential part of the healing process. But there has to be a "Yes, and" approach here to lead to greater healing. Yes, think and work through these questions, AND pair this wrestling with coping mechanisms and support. This links back to what many of the strategies in this book will point you to: surrounding yourself with things and people that uplift you, seeking counseling to navigate this journey, getting outside and exploring nature, getting creative, and getting connected to what matters most.

As we navigate our grief, these questions might never go away completely, but we can be assured that our faith and our life can withstand the storm. Our faith can handle the toughest of inquiries, and it can emerge from the wrestling match stronger and more resilient. We may not find all the answers we seek, but we can find peace in the journey and the knowledge that we are not alone in our search for understanding and never alone in our struggles.

PAUSE AND REFLECT:

Have you struggled to answer tough questions in the wake of your loss? What, if any, coping mechanisms have helped you "wrestle" with your questions so far?

Pass With Care

Today, on my way to work, I tried something new
I didn't turn on the radio or an audiobook
Or a podcast at one point five speed
per
   my
        norm

Today, I drove in silence, wrestling with thoughts
Sitting with my friends God and Gratitude
Passing road signs reminding me to go slow and
pass
   with
        care

Today, I saw the sunlight hitting the trees,
heard the hum of tires on the ribbon of road
And I wondered what it would be like if we all were
quiet
   more
        often

5

The Dumb Comments

f you have lost someone you love, I hate to say it, but you need to prepare for someone to inevitably say something to you that is so incredibly dumb you might want to punch them in the face (even if you are not the type of person who has ever wanted to punch anyone in the face before). You are going to want to ball up your fists and wallop them right in the jaw. You might also want to call them a bad name. I'm sorry, but that's just the truth. I'm not saying you'll do any of it, of course. But you'll want to, that's for sure.

These inane comments vary in their levels of stupidity, but you will think they are all stupid nonetheless. Here is a brief assortment of some of the dumb things you might hear, along with how you would like to respond in your head versus what polite company suggests would be an appropriate response. Yes, these things have been said many times to many different grievers, and many have been said to me. Read on after the table to find out the absolute number one dumbest comment someone ever said to me in the middle of my grief. It's a doozy.

Dumb Statement	What You Want to Say	What You Should Probably Say
"Everything happens for a reason."	"Really, Helen? Does it? This child was 12 and died by suicide/had cancer/was killed in a car accident. Do you really want to sit here and justify why it will all work out in the long run and what the reason for all of this will be? Screw you!" (Listen, I said we won't actually SAY these things, but don't act like you wouldn't think them, too. Even just a little bit.)	"It's hard to see what that reason might be at the moment, but I know you mean well." Then, walk away before either of you says anything else you would regret.
"They are in a better place."	"I don't want them to be in a better place. I want them healthy and whole and back in my arms." (Note: Although my faith is an important part of my life, and I also believe that my loved ones are in heaven (and, therefore, in a practical sense, a better place), I think it's bold to assume that everyone thinks this way. Know your audience and respect the belief systems of the person you are trying to comfort. For example, if they are atheists, they will not be comforted by this statement.)	"Thank you for being here." And then walk away before either of you say any other things you would regret.

"At least..." Note: fill in the blank with this one. "At least you had a long marriage." "At least you can still try for another child." "At least he didn't suffer long."	"SHUT UPPPPPP!"	Nod head halfway, not all the way like you're in total agreement, but a halfway nod, like, "Okay, let me think about this." There are no good verbal responses because the "at least" statements are the least helpful and most minimizing of all possible comments. Grievers hate this one, so it's best not to dignify it with any sort of verbal response.

Okay, are you ready for the dumbest of all the dumb comments ever said to me? I have this friend I've known since high school who has always been known for putting his proverbial foot in his mouth. He says the dumbest things on impulse without looking at the potential implications. He came to pay his respects at my mother's viewing. I was standing at her casket for the umpteenth time that day, quite numb and exhausted, looking at her, looking at the flowers, looking at the photos nearby. This friend stood next to me, taking it all in for a minute, and then turned to me and asked a question (mind you, there was no hint of malice or anything sinister with this).

"You know what I just realized?" he asked.

"What's that?" I replied.

"You're like... an orphan."

Wow, thank you so much for bringing that to light. Thanks for the reminder. I hadn't thought of that, seeing as how my dad has been gone since I was eight years old, and here I am at thirty-two, about to bury my mother. Thanks for making this clear to me, you big dumb dumb. I'm so glad you clarified that. *Insert all the sarcasm here.*

I don't even recall how I responded to him; I was just heavily annoyed in my state of exhaustion and grief. Yes, I am indeed an orphan. In a darkly humorous twist of events, my sister and I now frequently call each other on special days such as Mother's Day, Mom's birthday, etc., to say, "Hey, happy Thanksgiving/birthday/Mother's Day, ya orphan." And we can get a good laugh about it. But at the side of my mother's casket? Read the room, man. Read the room!

In summary, if people say something dumb to you in the wake of your loss, please know that you are not alone and that those of us who have walked the road ahead of you know what it was like to stand at that intersection. Keep walking. It is not worth your time or energy to craft some perfect response. You have so much else to process; do not waste any more time than absolutely necessary pondering someone's potentially well-intentioned but still hurtful words of "wisdom" or "comfort."

So often, people don't know what to say, so they word-vomit all over you in your time of need. These statements just pour salt into the wounds and make the healing process take that much longer. We have a few options when this happens. We can get mad at them for saying the wrong thing—and really, that may very well be justified. I probably could have slapped my friend right across the face or given him a glare with fire shooting out of my eyeballs, and I don't think many people would have blamed me. But we have other options in lieu of anger. We can hold on to that anger forever, or we can accept that they were coming from a place of trying to provide some modicum of comfort without really having a clue as to how. We can err on the side of grace. It is also important to remember that you can't control what anyone else says. You just can't. The only thing you can control is your response to what they say. Like we tell our young children on the playground or in the classroom, you cannot control other people's words or actions; you can only control what you do or say in response. Make good choices. Even when people are being dumb.

In the wake of grief, you will at some point be on the receiving end of some clumsy—if well-meaning—comments, just like that "orphan" remark. Staying angry about it does nothing to help our healing journey, and we don't want to let it distract us from that important work of growth and healing. It helps to remember that you are not alone in this; many have walked this part of the road before, and we understand the challenges. Keep moving forward. Don't stay stuck rehashing those remarks over and over for too long. There's more healing and hope to look towards, so look ahead and keep walking that road. You are not walking it alone.

PAUSE AND REFLECT:

Has anyone made an unkind but well-meaning comment to you since you lost your loved one? How did you respond? Would you do anything differently if you could go back and repeat the interaction?

Therapy

That pain in my chest, it still hurts,
But a lot of things have helped
Prayer, reading, writing,
And reading some more
Watching her favorites like
Beaches and The Sound of Music
Crying deep, heavy sobs
Laughing so hard it rattles my bones

The peonies blooming in my front yard
Taking a walk
Getting on an airplane
Setting boundaries
Bringing her favorite milkshake to the cemetery
Letting someone know when I'm down
Hugging my children
Looking at old photo albums

Breathing deeply
Being around other people
Being all by myself
Feeling mixed emotions and knowing that's allowed
Learning something new
Picking up something old
Knowing that I loved hard enough
To make it hurt this bad in the first place

6

The 100 Dreams

Books have always been a balm to my soul, the answer to most problems, and the comfort that I crave if I'm feeling out of sorts. The library has always been a place of peace, joy, and support throughout my life. As an adult navigating the loss of my mother, the feeling was no different. I felt that some of the answers to my problems could undoubtedly be found in a book, so off to the library I went. I checked out a memoir called *Hope's Boy*, filled with the details of another turbulent childhood with an imperfect mother and trauma in abundance. It reminded me of my own life and my own reconciliation with my mother, which thankfully happened before she passed. I checked out a few books on grief that unfortunately didn't help me much, and a book called *I Know How She Does It: How Successful Women Make the Most of Their Time* by Laura Vandercam. I didn't have hopes that this title would help me navigate my grief, but I was intrigued by the title and premise as a busy woman in general.

This was the book I happened to bring with me when visiting my best friend Amber in Atlanta for her birthday. She was a key crew member on a Godzilla movie that was being filmed, and while she thought she would have the weekend off while

I was there, she ended up having to work all day on Saturday. When she asked if I would mind coming along and essentially sitting all day while she worked, I jumped at the chance. It had been less than a month since Mom died, but I still had to care for my children and home and myself each day, be present at work, and generally get along in life while still operating under a heavy cloud of sadness. So if I had the chance to not only get a behind-the-scenes look at how a blockbuster is made, chat with a few crew and cast members, eat lunch from craft services, and also bring books and read for most of the day with no other responsibilities—sign me up. I was all in! Because it was such a unique setting, I can recall in vivid detail the pages I read that day out of *I Know How She Does It*. In it, Vandercamp details a thought exercise called the List of 100 Dreams, a bucket list of sorts. Essentially, it is a list of all the things you want to do, accomplish, or just want more of in your life. You write this list and then point your life and choices towards those list items. Call it goal setting, call it a bucket list, call it what you will, but it helps you be intentional with your life because one thing death teaches you is that life is precious, and we don't want to waste it.

The things on your List of 100 Dreams do not have to be big. They can be simple as long as they bring you joy. My list included plenty of big things but also simpler pursuits: "Burning scented candles. Reading more books. Jumping in leaf piles whenever the opportunity presents itself." Also, there do not *have* to be 100 things on this list. Just start writing, and it's okay if you end up with a dozen things on the list, or fifty, and not a full 100. Here is a sampling of what I wrote that day, sitting in an extra director's style chair on the set of *Godzilla: King of Monsters*, grateful to be there while still trying not to drown in grief caused by losing Mom. As you can see, some things were big, and some were small. I had a lot of time on my hands; it was a long day on set, so I got to almost seventy items that day and added more in the weeks that followed.

#12: See the Grand Canyon

#24: Watch more plays

#44: Make more family photo books

#51: More nature walks

#62: Jump in puddles or dance in the rain

#75: Go on a gondola ride in Italy

#95: Burn candles at home more often

The point of this list idea is to get you thinking about what you want more of in life. Think about it and start to make your own list. It's okay if it's wildly simple, wildly ambitious, or any-where in between. When we are intentional with our time, we can make better use of it and walk in deeper gratitude. The List of 100 Dreams helps the healing process as it helps you grab ahold of what you want *more* of in life and, conversely, helps you cut out what you want *less* of. When you curate your list of 100 Dreams, remember to not make it something that gives you stress or im-mense pressure; just use it as a guide to cultivate more joy and purpose in your life. Think about things that bring you joy and help you to feel the light.

Not only is the list an exercise about being intentional about adding things to your life that bring you joy, but it's also an exer-cise in thinking about what you do not want in your life, things that are toxic or harmful. You want to make the most of your one precious life. So think about that. What makes you come alive? Is there something you have always wanted to do but never have? What (within healthy, non-criminal parameters) do you want more of in your life? Think about it, find it, and get after it.

Our losses teach us that life is short and too precious to squan-der. None of us knows how much time we have, so treat time as the valuable commodity that it is. If you love flowers, plant them, or at least look at them at a local park or arboretum. If you love art, take a painting class. Walk around an art museum. Buy supplies to keep at home and use whenever you can find the time. Make the time. It will be worth it. If books fill your soul, go to a used bookstore, a new bookstore, or a library. Find a comfortable spot and flip the pages, letting the stories transport you somewhere new, even if it's only for ten dedicated minutes each day. Volunteer with a place of worship, charity group, or organization that means a lot to you or aligns with your most treasured values. See what's going on in your local community, think about how you can get involved, and then jump in. Watch trash TV (well, maybe not *too* often) or cat videos on YouTube if that fills your cup. Find simple joys. Bask in them. Live that one and only precious life of yours.

If you are stuck or unsure of what might bring you joy during this time, this would be a good thing to discuss with a trusted friend, family member, or therapist. Don't be afraid to try several things until you find what speaks to you. For inspiration, think about what you loved when you were a child. So often, what we loved back then might still stir up excitement and joy in our hearts now. As we grow, we tend to fall into the common trap of pushing hobbies and interests out of our lives and not making any time for them because of other responsibilities that come with adulthood like keeping up with housework, raising a family, building a career, or often all three at once. But think about what you used to love doing as a child. Were you always doodling or painting pictures? Did you love to dance? Did you spend all day outside with neighborhood kids, swimming, going for long bike rides, or building forts in the backyard? Is there a way to integrate any of that into your life now? When we fill our lives with things that breathe life into us, the result is that we feel more alive. What a tribute to those we have lost—to live a life where we feel alive. This list can add value and intentionality to your life and will help you in your healing journey.

It's like that quote on wooden plaques in home decor stores: "Life is too short for fake friends and fake cheese." Make sure you've got the good stuff. If something is dragging you down, chuck it. Replace the bad with things that uplift. It doesn't have to be huge, but it can be. The list is what you want it to be. You can accomplish your dreams, big or small, and a great place to start is by writing them down and giving them a place to live. That is the beauty of the list—it provides a place for your dreams to be. No matter how outlandishly large your goals, ambitions, desires, and wants might be, and no matter how seemingly insignificant they may be, write them down. See what happens. I'm thankful I have been able to accomplish some of the bigger items on my list, such as those that include travel, or the act of writing my first book. But the smaller items on my list matter, too. I wanted to light candles more often, and now I do. When I see a candle I love (or rather, smell a candle I love) at the store and my budget allows for it, I buy it with no second-guessing. I know it makes me happy. I know it's helping me cultivate a life of joy and fullness. And the peace and spiritual connection I get from lighting a wood-wick candle and watching it flicker is worth so much, no matter how small it may seem.

While we grieve the person or people we have lost, we honor them by living a life filled with the things that make *us* feel most alive. Let us embrace simple joys, reach for goals big and small, chase dreams, and, in doing so, find our own unique path to healing. Our dreams and joys deserve a place on our list. What a great way to hold dear to the memory of our people--by leaning into and celebrating the beauty of a life well-lived.

PAUSE AND REFLECT:

What would be on your List of 100 Dreams? What do you want more of? Smelling flowers? More color in your wardrobe? More lunch dates with an old friend? Finishing the degree? Getting sober? More forgiveness? Visiting Paris? Write it down and see where the intentionality takes you.

Questions to Ask God When I Get to Heaven

If we had gotten together for
Coffee and donuts
Like we said we should,
Would it have saved her life?

If I had sent her a text
Before she got in her car,
Would she have sat in the parking lot a minute longer
Blissfully unaware as she headed home,
Listening to her favorite emo songs,
That a drunk driver had missed her by two seconds?

Did he ask for me?
Did he wish I could have
been there to say goodbye?
And how many grains of sand and
Stars in the sky are there anyways?

7

The Shoulda Wouldas

I sent my old high school friend Ellen a Facebook message in early 2018 saying I noticed she was back in our hometown after living in another state for many years and that maybe we should get together for lunch and catch up. I noticed in the pictures she posted that she looked rail thin, her face gaunt, and I had a strong feeling something was wrong. Was she suffering a major health crisis? Disordered eating? I wasn't sure, but I wanted to connect. She didn't write back right away, and then Mom got so sick so fast that I stopped attending to my messages diligently. Ellen did eventually write back saying she'd love to get together: "When? Name the time!" she said. I never did name the time. I never got around to writing her back at all.

That summer, a local woman checked into a hotel in town, spent some time at the hotel bar, and then went back to her room, where she died by suicide. We all found out the next day in local news reports. That woman was Ellen. I found out that she had been battling a host of issues that maybe wouldn't have been helped by a cup of coffee with an old friend, but I couldn't help but wonder, what if it would have? What if I could have spoken some hope or joy into her life? What if I could have helped her consider a different path? Would it have made a difference? I hated that I didn't know. I regretted my inaction, and it brought back flashbacks of Angie's death. What if I would have called her that week? What if she had opened the funny article I had tagged her in while she was sitting in the parking lot at work before she had started to drive home? What if? What if? What if?

Maybe you have done this, too. Maybe you have almost driven yourself mad, wondering if anything you said or did or didn't say or didn't do would have changed anything. It's easy to get wrapped up in the "what ifs" and "should haves," but unfortunately, as we all know, those thought patterns do not change anything. You could spend literal years and so much energy mulling over countless scenarios, but it doesn't make a difference in the end. Your person is still gone; you do not get a do-over. You can't unscramble eggs once they have been whisked together. You can only figure out what to do from here on out.

Soon after Angie died, I talked with a coworker telling her how I felt about her death and wondering if I could have changed the outcome. She explained how she went through the same thought process after she lost her brother and that it did not help her feel better. It certainly did not bring him back. She further reminded me that beating herself up for what had happened, something completely outside her control, didn't honor him or his legacy, and it wouldn't honor Angie, either. And for you, dear reader, it won't serve you or your loved one to dwell on the "Oh, but if I had only done this" and "I should have done that" and so on. It can be a painful and ineffective rabbit hole down which to wander.

Think about it: would they want you to be blaming yourself and constantly rethinking how it could have gone differently? There are a million and one different "should have/could have" outcomes, but none of them bring your person back. Thinking of them on repeat is an exercise in futility. When you sense those familiar feelings creep up on you, shouting that you could have changed the outcome, resist the urge to give in and feel guilt or shame. Reframe your thinking into a resigned acceptance that what happened did ultimately happen, and the unfortunate truth is you can't go back and change history. You can only learn from it.

I didn't respond to Ellen's message, and I hate that. Of course, I wish I had, if only to see her and speak some joy or truth into her life over a plate of fries and a burger. But since I didn't and won't get the chance again, what can I do? I'll tell you what: I can be more intentional with the existing relationships I have right now. I can do my very best to text or message people back. If I'm thinking of someone, I can reach out to them at that very moment and let them know. If I run into an old friend and we say, "We really should get together sometime soon," and we both really mean it, then I should get my calendar out right then and there and write down a date and time. But what we don't need to do is spend any amount of time beating ourselves up over the coulda woulda shouldas of this life that we can't do anything about. Let's take any and all regrets and lay them down—kiss them goodbye.

A few practical exercises to help with this are as follows. Choose one, choose all, but they are tangible ways that you can practice the art of letting go and then move forward with more peace in your heart, knowing that you did the best you could with the information you had at the time and that it doesn't honor anyone's memory to continue beating yourself up over what wasn't said or done.

Idea 1: Write down your regrets on pieces of toilet paper. Yes, toilet paper. I know it might sound silly, but on each square, I might say something like, "I wish I would have written her back and met up for lunch," or "I wish I would have called Angie that night." Use as many squares as you need. Then, take them to the bathroom, drop them in the toilet bowl one by one, and flush them down the drain. Watch as they swirl. Say goodbye to the intrusive thoughts that don't solve anything. Let them stay down the drain, washed away.

Idea 2: Similar concept as idea number one, but instead of squares of toilet paper, write your regrets, your shoulda wouldas, on large pieces of paper. Use your normal handwriting, block lettering, fancy script—whatever you want to do. Then, find a safe location to have a small campfire and burn the papers. Watch the flames eat up the regrets and turn them into smoldering embers. If fire isn't an option, then rip the paper in half over and over again until there are hundreds of pieces and the letters are cracked apart. The words no longer exist. You can release them from your mental soundtrack. Let them burn. Let them go.

In my journey of grief, my Christian faith has been a source of comfort and strength. While I respect and love my readers of all faith backgrounds, I also want to share the ways in which my faith has been integral to this "letting go" process. If you believe in God as the Creator, the Alpha and Omega, you know that His strength is supreme. He is strong enough to carry all of my burdens—which is great because they are much too heavy to handle on my own. When considering all of the "should have" moments that pop up as we navigate our grief, it helps to remember God can make beauty from the ashes of any situation, no matter how dire. The unfortunate truth, however, is that in order for beauty to come from ashes, something has to burn in the first place.

We must also remember that we were never meant to carry those ashes, or in other words, our burdens and troubles, on our own. Lay them down at the cross. Say a prayer of "God, I need you in this moment. I am racked with guilt, regret, and remorse. These feelings are placing a huge burden on my heart. Please take these feelings away and replace them with a peace that surpasses all understanding. Carry these burdens; I lay them down at your feet. You are strong when I am weak. You will hold me up. What a comfort. I will forever thank you for sustaining me. Help me to forgive myself as you have forgiven me. In Jesus' name, I pray. Amen."

The written exercises are a tangible, visual way to allow your brain and heart to release these feelings of guilt over what happened and the questions of what might have been. The prayer is a cry to God to say, "I can't do this on my own—please take this guilt and regret from my heart and lips." Let these acts be a reminder that those regrets never serve you and don't have to hold you captive any longer. You have the power to release them. Let them go. Be free.

PAUSE AND REFLECT:

What regrets do you still hold onto that are robbing you of peace? Is there anything you need to let go of?

Birthday Lunch

I woke up in a tent, all that shared breathing
hanging in the air between myself and Chris and the kids.
Looked at my phone and saw the date, September 6th.
Happy birthday Mom, I whispered. Happy birthday.
You would be 71, celebrating with a salmon dinner
and maybe a rum and coke, light on the coke.
But you've been gone almost three years
And I'm celebrating you, without you.

Our friends were with us that day,
cooking up lunch at the campsite.
Beans and dogs, beans and dogs,
Who wants a piping hot helping of beans and dogs?
Luke cried from behind his camp stove
like a carnival barker.
My memories sparked like flint and steel.
I did. Me. Me. Ooh. Pick me.

I told him it was your birthday.
Told him you didn't cook much, but beans and dogs,
That was one of your specialties.
I filled up a bowlful. Sat in my camping chair.
Began to eat your birthday lunch.
It's a little easier this year than last year.
The ache isn't as strong.
There was peace. And in my head,
I said again, happy birthday, Mom.
I miss you, but I'm breathing.

8

The Triggers

Remember the shipwreck analogy from earlier and how it tells us grief will come in waves? I can confirm—that is the absolute truth. There are days that you know will be hard hitters, like holidays, birthdays, anniversaries. You see them looming on the calendar, and you have a visceral reaction: a sigh, a clenching of the jaw, a weight on your chest. They say you don't lose someone once; you lose them over and over again, with each wave that hits, with each painful reminder that they are gone. For me, St. Patrick's Day, the day Mom died, is a big trigger.

Erin Go Braugh and all that jazz—but to be honest, none of it resonates with me, and it makes me wonder: does anyone really care about ancestry or heritage at this point, or do they just want to wear green accessories and drink green beer? Do we really need clover and leprechaun displays in every major retail outlet for weeks leading up to it? And don't even get me started, as a parent of young children and an elementary school teacher to boot, on how much I do not have the mental or emotional bandwidth to set up leprechaun traps in my home or classroom and make a mess with green glitter. No. Absolutely not. I personally don't like glitter any day of the year, let alone on the anniversary of my mother's passing. Even if I hadn't suffered the greatest loss of my life on March 17th, using glitter is just taking things too far. I tend to avoid those green decor displays in the week leading up to St. Patrick's Day, and I especially did so in the first few years after Mom's death.

It should be said that if you love this day and love to go all out, please don't take this personally. My Irish friends, if you are out there, please know that I still love you and am not trying to ruin anyone's good time. Y'all can have green eggs or a green beer or wear green eyeshadow or whatever you want if it brings you joy. It is not my goal to rain on your parade. It's just that for me, the day is my least favorite of the year, and I try to stay away from all the St. Paddy's hoopla. Your triggers will be different than mine, as each experience is unique to the griever.

Simply put, a grief trigger is anything that acutely reminds you of a loss that has happened to you. As stated above, some are obvious, and you will be able to see them coming from a mile away, but some can hit you like a sucker punch out of nowhere. A grief trigger can come in the form of a song, sight, place, or even a specific smell. No matter what form it takes, it will likely elicit a powerful emotional response.

You can't always prepare yourself; year to year, they will change but know that they will inevitably come, and sometimes you will know it ahead of time. Adjust expectations according-ly. If something does catch you out of the blue, remember that it is a normal psychological and physiological response to feel sad or feel your chest tighten or your breathing become sharp. It is normal if it's been years since the loss, and you have a moment when the grief busts through the door and roundhouse kicks you in the stomach. There is nothing broken about this response. Like so much of the grief response, it is the price we pay for love.

I have always been a sucker for sad movies, and Mom and I loved the 1988 tear-jerker *Beaches* with Bette Midler and Barbara Hershey. There's a scene where the daughter of Barbara Hershey's character realizes that their hands look just alike. Soon after that, Barbara Hershey goes into this frantic search through photo albums and picture boxes because she wants to know if her own mother's hands looked the same as hers and her daughter's. Her own mother had passed away when she was little, and she never had the chance to check or ask while she was still alive.

I remember during one of our many viewings of this movie, Mom and I put our hands side by side and realized that ours looked just alike, too—same shape, same lines around the knuckles, same sensitivity to cold weather. I'm glad we thought to find this out when we did. This is a bit of a long way to bring you to what my own daughter asked me one night a few years after Mom died, but stick with me; it will make sense. We were making dinner, and she was telling me how they were learning about the "olden days" in social studies.

She giggled a little and asked, "Mommy, when Grandma Cam was a little girl, did she ever get spanked on the butt at school with a ruler?"

"Well, you know, I'm really not sure, baby. I don't think so... but maybe?" I answered.

And who knows exactly why, but just then, I felt the wind get knocked right out of my sails. I couldn't breathe. I had to wipe my face and sniff and choke back tears because I felt like it was such a silly little question to affect me so deeply. At that moment, I wished I could drive up to the nursing home or pick up the phone and say, "Hey, Mom, random question, but Evelyn wants to know if you ever got spanked with a ruler at school when you were little." I just wanted to know for sure. I wanted more information. More history. More stories.

But I couldn't get any of it. And it hurt so badly.

So, I turned to the next best things. That night, we called my sister to ask if she knew, but she wasn't sure, either. I could have read some of Mom's old journals, maybe flipping through them frantically like Barbara Hershey or lingering on each page instead, knowing that these words of hers are treasures. I could have browsed through old photo albums, not that there would be one of her getting the ol' ruler in grade school, but just to browse through the pages of history. I could look down at my hands. And maybe go hold them up to those of my children to see if they look alike, just so we all know.

If you're new at grieving or if you're a seasoned pro (what a rotten thing to be a pro at, I know, but I'm with you on that one, so at least we are in it together), just know that things can and will hit you out of nowhere. And when it does happen, it's okay to sit in the grief. It's okay to feel it bubble up through your heart and leak out of the corners of your eyes. It's okay to hold space for all the emotions that you need to feel. Honor it, and remember that you are not alone in it. Here, we'll link hands and keep moving forward together.

Even though we can't always prepare ourselves, there are some proactive steps we can take to deal with some of the more common grief triggers. Next, we will dive into three helpful steps you can take to cope with some of the more common and obvious triggers, such as anniversaries, birthdays, Mother's Day, Father's Day, etc.

STRATEGY ONE: AVOID ISOLATION

If you know a difficult date is coming up, make a plan to be distracted and/or be with someone on that day. It can help you preemptively avoid feelings of isolation or loneliness on what you are expecting to be a very tough day. Everyone is different, but you may want to do something to celebrate the life lived. Maybe if it's Mother's Day and you are grieving the loss of your mom, you can get together with a sibling or your own child and make your mom's favorite dinner. Hold space for your loved one on this special day and let other people in. You may just want to be alone, and that's okay, too. But at least let someone in through calling, FaceTiming, or texting.

STRATEGY TWO: ACKNOWLEDGE WHAT IS HAPPENING

It can be daunting and stressful to relive grief all over again, especially when it hits you seemingly out of nowhere, but if you understand where it comes from and you are mentally primed for the myriad emotions you'll experience, you will be better prepared to handle the grief triggers when they arise. It doesn't serve you well to act like it's not happening or the trigger doesn't exist. As mentioned earlier, honor those emotions when they arise, but know that they will pass. Breathe deeply. Talk about it. Write about it. Acknowledge and accept the difficulty because just by acknowledging your feelings, you are one step closer to processing the grief and moving forward in a healthy manner.

STRATEGY THREE: HAVE A FLOOD MANAGEMENT PLAN (OR MULTIPLE)

When we go back to our trusty shipwreck analogy, we remember that sometimes those waves hit us out of the blue—a smell, a song, driving through a certain town, walking into a certain place. You might have already known that grief triggers were a thing, but after reading this chapter, you now know with certainty. So, what are we going to do? We are going to have a few Flood Management Strategies for when this inevitably happens. Have a few coping mechanisms on standby for when something triggers you (more on this later, but this would be a great topic to flesh out in greater detail with a licensed professional counselor or therapist). Those coping mechanisms could include calming breathing exercises, going for a walk or hike, listening to a certain song that calms you down or puts you in a good mood, working on some sort of creative pursuit, etc. Being proactive about it can help you better handle those grief triggers when they do flood in. Having coping mechanisms on standby is like having flood insurance.

Just like I look away from the St. Patrick's Day displays and the shamrock shakes at McDonald's (how ironic that she loved those things as much as she did), now is a good time for you to think about things that may be grief triggers for you. It helps to proactively prepare for them when you can and to be gentle with yourself when they come up unexpectedly. Half the battle is realizing that it is happening and acknowledging it, and that alone is enough to survive it. When you feel that flood of emotions, it would be a good time to stop and pray for peace and wisdom to navigate the situation. To breathe deeply. Inhale. Exhale. Repeat. Start small and take things one moment at a time. This is normal, and you are not alone.

PAUSE AND REFLECT:

What triggers might you anticipate? What can you do to protect your peace when those triggers inevitably arise?

PART 2

HEALING

Baby Steps

Somebody gave us a gift card
to Leo's Coney Island
We went there about a week
after Mom's funeral.
I was still walking in a fog.
Nothing was funny yet.
But I stole a bite of Jackson's
pancakes, and they were delicious.
I got a tuna melt with pickles
and it was toasted just right.
The kids were pulling silly faces
and Chris met us there after his college class
I said who's that handsome guy walking in,
like I really didn't know
it was my own husband,
and the kids laughed.
I smiled,
and the pit in my stomach
was still there, still heavy,
but maybe a few ounces of it
dissolved right then.

9

The Helpers

In the summer of 1994, I was eight years old and newly father-less. Dad had died that May, and even though he and Mom had been separated for a while before that, his permanent absence was still felt deeply. Mom and I were figuring out how to keep moving forward, which was hard because even when I was little, I so often felt that I had to be the grown-up while Mom was navigating the ups and downs of her mental health struggles. There were helpers who made us feel seen, though, and I will always appreciate that. My second-grade classmates made me cards, complete with spelling mistakes you would expect from that age group, with sentiments such as, "Dear Christina, I am sorry your dad did" and "Dear Christina, I'm sorry your bab bibe." There were my maternal grandparents, who would take me for week-ends at a time or longer in the summer, making sure I was fed and tucked in at night. Mom was in such a state of shock, and her mental state was delicate even in the best of times, so this sent her reeling. It was hard for us to create any positive memories during this time. One, however, sticks out vividly.

Dad had always worked blue-collar jobs as a line cook in restaurants or in a newspaper factory and did not have life insurance when he passed. However, my Mom got a sum of Social Security money after he died, and with some of the money, she decided to make a purchase that she had been talking about for a long time but had never been able to make: a boombox. For anyone under the age of thirty who may not know what I am talking about, it's what we used to use in the "olden days" when we wanted to listen to music. And this one was epic. It only had room for one CD at a time, as the 3 and 5 disc changers were not as popular yet, but it also had an AM/FM radio setting, a dual cassette deck, and two huge speakers that could be detached (to a certain distance) to create a surround sound effect. She bought it at Kmart, a big box retailer that was the go-to store in our rural town.

Mom let me choose a CD of my very own. I picked the Ace of Base album, *The Sign*. Mom picked a few and, in the months that followed, acquired many more: Mariah Carey, Whitney Houston, Anita Baker, The Beach Boys, Elvis, and Frank Sinatra. An eclectic mix of music began to blast from that thing nonstop, a constant background soundtrack to our daily lives. She was so proud of that boombox, so happy to own it. It was a positive amongst the pain.

Fast forward to almost twenty-five years later: when mom was in hospice, the nurses reminded us many times about hearing being the last sense to go and to keep talking, to play music, and she would hear it. I don't know why I hadn't thought of that sooner. I flashed back to that boombox and recalled how central it was to our lives.

I went on a lengthy hunt around town for a CD player and CDs Mom would like. That old boombox had long since been gone. I could have gone more modern with a Bluetooth device or something, but I knew it had to be a CD player. Looking back, it was about control, about completing a concrete mission. I couldn't control what was happening to Mom overall, but Lord help me, I would find some compact discs!

I remember when there were two full aisles of CDs in that Kmart, every genre you could think of. Now, as I hunted for what I needed, there was no more Kmart (they had closed our town's location along with hundreds of others a few years before), no more CDs or players save for a microscopic section at the third local store I checked (mission accomplished!), and soon, there would be no more Mom. I was struck by all of this after I finally found a collection of Frank Sinatra's greatest hits, which was perfect for her.

The music played softly by her bed as I sat down beside her, keeping vigil, resting my eyes but not my mind. *Ding*, I heard my phone ping. It was my friend Rachel texting to say, "A lot of us want to help you. What would be most helpful? What do you need?" That was a loaded question, one I wasn't sure how to answer.

Could I say I needed a time machine so I could take back any mean thing I ever said to my mother? Can you please rewrite my past so I understood her mental illness sooner, as a child, as a teenager, maybe, so I didn't spend so much time being angry with her? Could you clone me so I could be present for my mother, my husband and children, and myself—all at the same time? I was humbled and grateful for the offer but also not used to accepting help. I like control and concrete missions, remember?

I thought of the most practical and also most needed thing: food. "Thank you so much. Maybe meals? I can't even think of cooking right now." Rachel wrote back quickly, "We're on it. If you have any favorites, dislikes, or allergies, just let me know." By the end of the day, she had set up a meal train that would keep us fed for the next two weeks. I was further humbled when meals were delivered, and I don't think I'll ever forget a single one. Jill, who had lost her husband two years before, dropped off all the fixings for taco night. Michele brought milk, orange juice, and breakfast foods. Tonia dropped off an Italian feast and proved without a shadow of a doubt that sometimes Jesus shows up to earth disguised as a pan of lasagna. When I got home and saw it, after a long day of putting together the photo boards for the funeral home, I ate it right out of the pan.

I'll also never forget my college roommate Kirsten showing us love in a tangible way. I didn't ask her to, didn't tell her to—she just let me know one day when we were right in the thick of it that she was on her way to my house and was dropping off paper plates, plastic silverware, and some frozen meals. I was so struck by this. Kirsten had three young children at home, including her infant twin boys, a full-time job, and she lived an hour and a half away. Yet she still got in the car and drove. After stopping at my house, since she was so close to the nursing home, I asked her to stop by so I could give her a hug and say thank you in person. I don't remember what was said, but I remember she sat next to me on a moderately comfortable floral sofa in the common area near Mom's room and listened while I let words fly out of my mouth. The listening meant so much. It all meant so much.

I don't take it for granted that I had people willing to step in and help us. I understand that may not be everyone's story. I am forever thankful it is part of mine. What the taco night, pan of lasagna, and paper plates all had in common was they all worked together to teach me to set aside my pride and accept help. As a child, I experienced massive instability and trauma, even if it took me decades to realize that's what it was called. I had to be independent from a young age, never knowing what mood Mom would be in or if she'd remember to pay the bills that month or go grocery shopping. I thought all of that was normal.

When I graduated high school, the parents all sent in little sentiments or well wishes to be placed next to our senior yearbook photos. I wrote mine myself because Mom was in a depressed state. I made sure to hype it up and include plenty of positive adjectives so the rest of my graduating class would know how my Mom felt about me: "Christina, I am so proud of the beautiful, smart, funny, hardworking woman you have become. Love, Mom."

All of this led to an independence that served me well in some ways but could also turn into a fault when I took it too far. As a young adult, I could be drowning, and the farthest I might go would be to sputter, "Excuse me, if you don't mind, if it wouldn't be too much trouble, do you think you could throw me a buoy? If not, though, it's totally okay." That's where I was mentally throughout raising my three young children and most of the caretaking for my mom.

But when she was on her deathbed and people were reaching out saying, "What can we do?" it broke something open within me. People wanted to help. They wanted to shine a light into our darkness. And by never accepting it, never reaching out for it, I would be denying them the chance to use their gifts, time, talents, or resources to help someone. So I let them in, and it taught me, assisted me, and helped me to see the light shining through in an otherwise very dark time.

I think of a dear friend of mine who, at the time of my mother's death, did not have a lot of financial bandwidth. Spending extra money on a meal or a gift card would not have fit comfortably into her budget. But I will never forget her kindness in coming to my house the day of my mother's funeral, helping my daughter, who was five years old at the time, get ready in her dress, tights, and fancy shoes, and doing her hair for me. I still tear up thinking of how much it meant to me. That whole day was such a whirlwind, and I was so sad and overwhelmed. It meant so much to me that my daughter's hair looked so precious and that my friend went out of her way to show that kindness to us. If I had put up a wall or told her no, don't worry about it, it wouldn't have solved anything, and it would have prevented my friend from being able to use one of her talents in a very sweet and special way.

It's so easy to fall into the "I'll just do it myself" trap.

I can do it on my own.

I am strong.

I am capable.

I don't need anyone.

This turns us into over-stressed martyrs—so is it really the best way? Is it the only way? No. Whether someone is overtly asking, "What can I do to help?" or they show up at your doorstep with a casserole, we should accept it and simply say, "Thank you." If someone is drowning, a loud and desperate "Help!" shouted into the surrounding area would be more effective than a whispered, "Um, excuse me, could you maybe give me a hand here? If it's not too much trouble. If not, though, it's totally okay." Your life is worth saving. Your sanity is worth saving. If you need to ask for or accept help, understand that it is not weak. It does not mean you are less than or feeble. It means you are self-aware, you understand your own limitations, strengths, and weaknesses, and you are brave.

I think of that little eight-year-old version of me, picking out the Ace of Base CD, jamming out to it, and so many others back at home. I think of that big boombox and how it brought us joy and connected us when so many other things divided and frustrated us. I'm glad that little girl doesn't know yet about the other CD player, the one she finds twenty-four years later, to provide Mom some modicum of comfort on her deathbed. Little Christina had enough to handle already. But I wish I could tell her that she doesn't have to handle it all on her own. And neither do you.

PAUSE AND REFLECT:

How do you feel when you think about asking for or accepting help from others? Can you think of a time when someone helped you and it impacted your life or grief process in a positive way?

Sweetness and Thorns

It happened again
Eating a raspberry
from my very own garden
And I thought of you
Can you believe it?
I have some of my very own?
It used to be you and me
But after all these years
You're still gone
And every bite reminds me of
All you taught
The weeds are overgrown
The berry bushes need to be thinned
How do I do it all?
I paid attention when you did it
But we still didn't get enough time

10

The Senses

I was about six years old, helping Grandpa pull out the weeds growing on the large brick patio in the backyard. I loved to spend time outside at Grandma and Grandpa's house, helping him maintain the patio, work in his garden, or rake leaves. On our knees, hands in the dirt, Grandpa would teach me how to use a little trowel, trusting me with the tools from a young age, showing me how to grip as low as I could on any invasive weeds, yanking them out by the roots and giving them a good, hearty shake to remove the excess soil before putting them in the pile to be burned later.

He always let me help and was always so patient with me, not minding if I worked much slower than he did, telling me, "Every little bit helps, Punkin' Seed," using the special name he only used for me. He spent those days telling me about the different types of tomatoes and why he had to tie the plants to the wooden poles in the ground, telling me how to thin out the raspberry bushes and watch out for poky parts, and telling me nothing at all, just working together in the dirt and the silence. He tended to that garden beautifully, and it was one of my favorite places in the world. It was a 20x20 square of perfection. Now that I'm grown, I realize he must have loved and cherished those moments as much as I did, but now I am the sole keeper of those memories.

In the raspberry patch, I would carry a small wooden quart container and try to fill it as best as I could. The raspberries would later be sprinkled onto a dish of vanilla ice cream after dinner that night or in a jam expertly made by Grandma. But on more than one occasion, after being out there for what seemed like hours, I returned to the house with barely a smattering of berries in my container. "Where are all the raspberries?" Grandma asked me. I caught Grandpa's twinkling eye as he stood behind Grandma. He knew. I looked sheepish and told Grandma, "In my belly!" Instead of bending towards firmness, per her usual, she softened and smiled at me, laughing at my response.

Now, at my own home, I have a raspberry patch. Several years ago, a family friend was thinning out her garden and gave me several raspberry plants. As I planted them in my backyard, I thought about Grandpa and all he taught me. I thought about his patience, his love, his wisdom. I thought about Grandma's jam on toast in the morning, the dishes of vanilla ice cream at night, and the mostly empty wooden containers during the long, delightful summer days. I am not as skilled of a gardener as Grandpa was, and I wish he and Grandma were still here to answer my questions about what flowers or vegetables to plant, when, and where to buy the seeds. Google is a blessing to my generation, but it doesn't come close to replacing the ability to call Grandma and Grandpa. All these years later, it still hurts not to be able to pick up the phone and call them.

It's amazing how little moments, sights, sounds, and tastes can release a flood of memories. They can be very therapeutic or very triggering, depending on the memory in question. A certain smell, touch, taste, sound, or sight can take you back to an exact moment, and sometimes, it's traumatic and should be avoided, so be kind to yourself if you come in contact with something that affects your senses in a difficult way.

Sometimes, however, it is beautiful and cathartic and should be embraced. At first, you may look at it with profound sadness, but eventually, it will be more bittersweet or even make you smile. Trust the process.

Goodale's Bakery in Grayling, Michigan, is easy to pass by. It's a block off the main road that runs through the same northern Michigan town where Grandpa would always stop for groceries before getting to his vacation cabin in Traverse City. He would always stop at this bakery on every trip up north unless we were driving through on a Sunday because they were closed. He'd get a few types of bread, coffee cakes, cookies—he always had a bit of a sweet tooth. He'd chat with the baker, Mr. Goodale himself, as his goods were rung up. Many years after his death, my husband and I were driving up to northern Michigan with our kids for a family weekend away when it dawned on me that we'd be driving through Grayling and maybe we should make a special pitstop.

I hadn't been there since I was a teenager, on what would ultimately be my last trip up north with Grandpa (side note: that is another profound fact that I think about sometimes—there will come a time when it is your last time doing a certain tradition with your loved one, and you don't even realize it will be the last time. Even more of a reason to walk in deep gratitude for every moment we have and appreciate the little things in life). We Googled to confirm that the bakery was still open, and it indeed was, so we stopped. I was not prepared for the feeling I'd get when I walked in. Talk about a grief trigger.

The smell, the look, the feel of the railing I held as I walked up the two steps to the main floor was overwhelming—and even more, the smell. It was like I was a kid again, and Grandpa was right behind me, about to say his oft-repeated line, "You tell me if you see anything you'd like, and we'll get it." But he wasn't there, only in spirit. I was the grown-up this time. I felt tears spring to my eyes as I looked at all the goods on display—the bread, the donuts and pastries behind the glass, the bags of cookies, and the coffee cakes. They were all exactly the way I remembered. It was overwhelming, and I just let the emotions happen. I mentioned to the cashier that this place was special and why, and she smiled kindly and said she was glad to hear that, but I don't think she actually understood the depth of my feelings. We've stopped several times since. I even bought a hoodie with their logo to commemorate my visits there, and I don't cry anymore upon walking in. But I still remember and feel like Grandpa is right there behind me, encouraging me to pick out a treat and live life indulging in that sweet tooth when the occasion calls for it. I'm grateful for his legacy in so many ways, for the traditions he started that I get to continue. A wild thought, really; did he know he was creating a legacy when he was just living his life? Do any of us realize that the regular stuff of life, or the traditions we impart, will become treasured keepsakes one day in the hearts of our loved ones? Maybe we should think about that more. Maybe we should treasure them ourselves while we are still here and value the extraordinary nature of events that otherwise seem commonplace.

Your memories and senses have the power to transport you and are a way of keeping memories alive. As previously mentioned, they can be triggering in difficult ways, but they can also trigger feelings of gratitude, joy, childlike innocence, and happiness. Like so much of the grief journey, it will often be a mixture of more than one emotion. Walking into Goodale's that first time as an adult reminds me of the scene at the end of the Pixar movie *Inside Out*. The final scenes center around Riley, an eleven-year-old girl, as she returns home after running away. Throughout the film, the audience is taken on an emotional journey inside Riley's mind, where personified emotions—Joy, Sadness, Anger, Fear, and Disgust—control her actions and thoughts.

Towards the end, Joy, the exuberant and positive emotion, comes to understand the importance of Sadness. Joy realizes that Sadness plays a crucial role in Riley's emotional well-being, as it allows her to connect with others, seek help, and process her complex feelings. The lesson here is that it's okay to experience sadness and that it's a normal part of life. In another pivotal moment at the end of the film, Joy embraces Sadness and allows her to take control of Riley's emotions during a crucial situation. When Riley returns home and opens up to her parents about her struggles and feelings of missing her old life since moving to a new state, it demonstrates the significance of communication and expressing emotions openly. The movie reminds us that sharing our feelings with loved ones is essential, and doing so can lead to understanding and support. Furthermore, the movie imparts a lesson in acknowledging and appreciating the entire spectrum of emotions, not just the positive ones. It's not feasible to experience only joy one hundred percent of the time, nor is it possible or recommended to experience only sadness all the time either—nor any one singular emotion for that matter. Sometimes, what triggers a sensory response will give us a variety of emotions all at once.

Often, it is a sight, smell, sound, or taste that can transport you back in time, for better or worse. Even long after we say goodbye to the ones we love, we are still connected to them through the senses that evoke so many memories. The sensory details that hit us as we move forward serve as our bridge to the relationships we shared and the memories we made. They help us tell the stories of our past while weaving them together with the reality of our present and future. They can help us on our journeys as we find simple but impactful ways to keep our loved one's memory and spirit alive.

PAUSE AND REFLECT:

What sensory details take you back or evoke strong memories of your loved one?

Passed and Present

Her divinity frosting
The way she said hello
Almost British,
When she answered the phone

His thirst for knowledge
The way he would always
In the shadows,
Give and help and pour out

Her insatiable sweet tooth
The way she sang
Incorrectly, mind you
The lyrics to every song

Memories live on.
Legacies get passed down.
Is anyone ever really gone?

11

The Ways to Honor Their Memory

My mom was never much of a cook. I can count on my fingers the number of meals she made when I was younger. Let me do a mental exercise and see if I can list ten:

- *Plain salmon*
- *Buttered noodles*
- *Goulash* (if you know, you know)
- *Stouffer's Lasagna*
- *Stouffer's Stuffed Green Peppers*
- *Stouffer's French Bread Pizzas*

I can't even get to ten, but I can add at least one more dish: cranberry sauce. At Thanksgiving, she would always make the cranberry sauce, the one made by following the recipe on the back of the bag of fresh cranberries. Grandma Conde would make everything else, but Mom would bring cranberry sauce in a special glass dish with a beautifully scalloped edge.

As the first round of holidays without my mom approached, I was practicing the art of naming my feelings, and the night before Thanksgiving, I felt... sad. I was in my kitchen, making that simple cranberry sauce, but it didn't seem so simple in the moment. Sure, there was nothing fancy about it. A bag of whole cranberries plus a cup of water plus a cup of sugar. We were never interested in fancying it up, no orange zest or apple bits or anything else. Easy. No fuss. This cranberry sauce was just about the only uncomplicated part of my mother there was. It has always been my favorite part of the meal. When I was younger, I loved the flavor of it mixing with a bite of turkey at the same time. Now that I'm grown, I still love it for that reason, but also because it makes me think of her.

That November, I knew I had loads to be thankful for, but it was okay to have sadness mixed in, too. Grief doesn't care what day of the year it is or if you have a lot going on. Grief is a bear who is always ready to wrestle with you. Sometimes, you can kick it in the chest and move on with your to-do list, and other times, it pins you to the ground. Making that cranberry sauce, I was feeling pinned down. At that moment, I wasn't sure if the holidays would get easier with each passing year or if they would get more difficult. I didn't know the end game, how it all would play out. I just knew that it made me feel a tiny bit better talking about it and naming my bear. That day it was called cranberry sauce, made the way she used to make it, in the dish she always put it in.

The holidays are rough for those of us who are missing someone. Let's be honest: all days are rough for those of us who are missing someone. The holidays are especially tricky, though, because there is such a mixture of emotions. The days may be filled with a mix of gratitude and peace and light and good things, but also, at the very same time, a whole lot of heartache. Maybe it will help you, too, to talk about it, write about it, and acknowledge it. What do you miss the most? Was it her gravy? His prayer before dinner? Her yearly desire to drive around all the neighborhoods with the best Christmas light displays? His insistence on getting both turkey legs? Her tradition of taping a candy cane to every single Christmas present? His loathing of Black Friday? For me, that first Thanksgiving, my bear, the thing that brought me back, was a pack of cranberries with some water and some sugar.

But it was not just a bear. It was not only something to be feared or saddened by. In fact, the things that tug at us in regard to their memories are also the things that can be used to honor our loved one's legacy. Yes, making that silly, simple recipe made me sad, but it also connected me to her. When I make this simplistic side dish, I feel close to her. In this small way, I keep her memory alive. It made me feel good to carry on with something that my mom had started. My kids don't even put it on their plates because they don't like it, but that doesn't stop me from teaching them the recipe and having them help me with it. It is a way to honor my mom and her quirkiness. I could not count on her for everything, but we could count on her for this contribution, and I'm going to keep that torch aflame.

Think about the person you miss and imagine something you can do to keep their memory alive in ways that make sense to you. Maybe it is continuing an old tradition. Maybe it's starting a new one. A friend's mother always wanted to travel more, and after she died, this friend decided to take her ashes with him on his many motorcycle trips and spread them all over the United States. A woman in my town tragically lost her toddler daughter, Lily, at the hands of an abusive stepmother, and she has since channeled her grief and energy into creating a non-profit organization called Justice for Lily. This organization does incredible work to advocate for children who have been through abuse, to raise awareness and preventive education, and through their fundraising efforts, have provided Christmas presents for hundreds of Michigan children who are in the foster care system.

For several years, I ran an annual 5K called AdvoKate, started by a husband and wife team who lost their daughter Kate to brain cancer. Each year before the race, they spoke about how they chose this town and course specifically because it was full of so many hills—the ups and downs of the race course mirrored the hills and valleys of Kate's journey while undergoing treatment. On the 20th anniversary of my dad's death, I ran my first half marathon. I had not considered myself a runner until about a year prior when I had decided to make some positive changes to feel healthier after our daughter was born. I wanted to prove to myself and my children that I would do whatever I could to keep myself healthy and there for them for as long as possible if I had any say in the matter.

My dad, unfortunately, did not take good care of his body, and he died of heart failure at age 48. The years of heavy smoking, poor eating habits, and lack of exercise caught up with him, and it made me so sad to think that he might not have missed everything if he had made different choices. He may have been able to walk me down the aisle and meet his grandkids. But then again, you never know how things might have turned out differently, and it's not helpful to go too far down those rabbit holes. At any rate, I wanted to do the half marathon to remember him, release my frustrations over what "could have been," and acknowledge that while I can't change the past, I can change my own choices and affect the future. After Angie died, Amber, our friend Grace, and I organized a scholarship fund in her name. Those are all just some examples of ways a loved one's memory could be honored.

Make no mistake, though—the way you honor your loved one does not have to be grand. It just has to be meaningful to you. When I visit my mother's grave on Mother's Day or a random Thursday, I usually play the song we played at her funeral, the song that perfectly summed up her personality as someone who definitely marched to the beat of her own drum, to say the least: *My Way* by Frank Sinatra, with smoothly crooned lyrics explaining that he did things in his own unique way, just like Mom did. In that moment, at her graveside, I honor her.

Just placing the framed picture of my grandparents I have hanging up by the stairway in my home honors them. There are so many things you can do: playing a certain song every time you drive back to your hometown, getting a tattoo (yes, I suppose that would be parked in the "grand gesture" category), writing a memoir to be published, writing memories in a journal just for you, hosting an event, watching their favorite movie every year on their birthday, fundraising for a cause that mattered to them, painting a room a certain color because you both loved it, or visiting a place you always said you would visit together. There are so many ways to go about this, and it's up to you. But doing *something* that will honor your loved one and preserve their memory is a way to bring healing to your heart after the loss. It can be grand or simple, but it should honor them in some way and bring you peace. Death ends a life, but not the love felt for that person and not the bond you shared. The love keeps going and lives on in the many ways you choose to honor your person. In some scenarios, everyone will know about your chosen way to memorialize your loved one's legacy. In other scenarios, you will be the only one who knows. In both, their memory lives on.

PAUSE AND REFLECT:

Think of the person you are missing. What is something, big or small, you can do to honor their memory this year?

Therapy 2.0

I sank into the couch
Took a deep breath
Sent a text to Amber.

I think it's time, I said.
I'm going to make an appointment
To talk to someone.

Her reply came quickly,
Just one perfect line—
I AM SO PROUD OF YOU.

12

The Therapeutic Pursuits

Reading books, such as the one you are holding right now, to help you work through your grief is a wonderful pursuit. Do it as often as you need to. While I hope this book helps you immensely, it likely will not be the only one you read during this season. Furthermore, I am not a trained mental health professional, nor a counselor or therapist—and I do not claim to be one. I'm a woman who has been punched time and time again by the fists of loss, like Rocky Balboa in the ring, and still survived the fight. I have words to share and lessons learned, but if the pit of grief is deep and you are finding yourself lost, consistently dark, or continually struggling, please consider talking through your feelings with a trained professional. Problems fester in the dark and die in the light. Talk about them. Talk about the person you miss. Let a professional guide you through the trauma and work through it, bringing you a greater sense of healing.

About two months after Mom died, I was still wrecked. I was going about my daily business wearing a mask, and this was pre-pandemic, so no, not *that* kind of mask. I would smile, run errands, and teach my students. I would make dinner and take the kids to baseball practice, trying my best not to place my burden of pain on their little shoulders.

However, I also had cracks, moments of great impatience or frustrations, moments when I took it out on my kids and snapped over household issues that really weren't that big of a deal but seemed monumental to me. I knew I was off. I knew I was in a pit of sadness. I felt like a large part of my identity as mom's daughter and caregiver was gone. I had been fatherless since I was eight years old, but I had always had my wildly imperfect, quirky, and mentally unstable mother. I always took care of her. I always knew I could visit her, even during the years in which the visits were strained, and she would want to know what was going on in my life. But now, I was, as my friend so bluntly put it at Mom's funeral, an orphan.

I felt every bit the part. My faith tells me I have a heavenly Father, a God who loves me, and I do not want to minimize that because it is important to me and comforts me to remember that. But at the same time, losing both of my earthly parents by the age of 32 really wrecked me. My identity as a daughter felt so cracked. I knew I needed to work through this and couldn't do it on my own. My husband was a great support during this time, but he was also traveling a lot for work and was frequently out of state for weeks at a time. During one such period, after the kids went to bed, while my house was silent but my mind racing, I texted Amber and told her I was going to call a few places the next day to set up an appointment with a therapist. She texted back immediately, in all caps: "I AM SO PROUD OF YOU." The perfect reply.

Maybe you've been taught to stuff your emotions away and that revealing them, seeing them, feeling them, talking about them, and/or working through them is wrong or a sign of weakness. My maternal grandmother, Grandma Conde, was like this to a T. She almost always had only one expression: stoicism. She was a stern, no-nonsense woman raised on a working farm in the

1920s and 30s (so post World War I) and right in the middle of the Great Depression. She was too busy working her proverbial tail off on the farm to make time for frivolous things like emotions. I can only imagine how difficult it was for her after my mother was born when she suffered from severe postpartum depression. My mother was born in 1949, and instead of therapy and unpacking your emotions in a healthy way, something that was very on-trend in mental health circles at that time was a practice called Electroconvulsive Therapy. ECT worked by using electricity to induce seizures in a patient.

This practice, invented in the 1930s, was widely used in the 1950s through the 1970s to treat mental health disorders. A doctor would use electrical pulses to induce seizures, which were believed to reorient the brain's neurological pathways and treat mental health conditions such as depression and bipolar disorder. This was right at the precipice of medications for mental health conditions being widely available. For some people, ECT may have worked. It has long been marked with controversy and debate. For Grandma, it did *not* work. It may have caused temporary respite, but it also altered her personality so much that family lore tells us though she used to be giggly and light, she became much more rigid and firm and never really went back to her old self. She spent many years self-medicating with Old Forester whiskey and still kept most of her emotions under wraps. A prime example of this is when Grandpa came into the kitchen crying after receiving news from a relative in his home state of Missouri. "Oh, come on, John," she said, chastising him for crying and "making a fuss." He had just found out that his sister died! There was simply no space held for feelings. Grandma, while admittedly having a soft spot in her heart for me, the baby of the family, could also be characteristically cold to the rest of the family.

So yes, perhaps you grew up thinking that traditional talk therapy is not for you, you don't need it, and it won't help. Maybe it's because you are tough and don't need to bother yourself with all that chit-chat and frilly, emotional stuff. Maybe you were brought up in a religious environment that told you you just need to pray harder. Maybe you were told God will take care of your emotions, and if you are still feeling sad, it has nothing to do with your trauma or your brain chemistry; you're just not praying hard enough. While prayer has a beautiful place in a healthy faith dynamic, I have to go on record as saying that's all a crock of bull. Some of the most faithful people I know have experienced trauma, mental health crises, or physical health tragedies, no matter how hard or how often or how genuinely they prayed. Include prayer in your treatment plan by all means if your faith plays an important role in your life, but go beyond it as well. Think of the phrase "Yes, and," as in, yes, prayer is powerful, AND it can be coupled with other proactive measures. Yes, faith can be integral to your healing, AND so can therapy. Therapy does not mean you are weak or incapable of handling life's problems and losses on your own. It means the opposite. It builds strength, resilience, and fortitude. It helps you unpack the trauma of the loss you have experienced. It is not weak to work with a personal trainer if you want to tone your muscles. It is not weak to work with a business mentor if you want to grow your entrepreneurial skills. It is not weak to consult an orthopedic specialist when you sprain or break a bone. Similarly, it is not weak to seek support from a mental health professional when you are going through a difficult season of life (or even as a preventative measure when you are *not* going through a difficult season of life).

In my first therapy session, I gave a bird's eye view of my life up to the point when my mom died. I entered the foster care system at age four, and all of us siblings were separated for good when I was five. My dad died when I was eight, and I was raised by my mom alone while she fought her battles against mental illness. I lost my grandparents as I entered early adulthood and became my mom's legal guardian when I was 21. Recently, I lost her to colon cancer. Then, at the next session, the therapist said, "Which part of the trauma do you want to unpack first?" and I'm not kidding; I was so confused.

What do you mean? Trauma?! I just thought those were normal life experiences. Oh... Trauma. You know, that makes a lot of sense. Wow. It had honestly never occurred to me before that my life had so much trauma. I thought it was just... life. Doesn't everyone deal with some level of anguish or upheaval in life? This is just par for the course, right? It was such a huge, eye-opening, revelatory experience to give a name to what I had experienced. Just that key takeaway helped so much, and in later sessions, he continued to help me unpack it all and give voice to some lingering frustrations, as well as helpful strategies for moving forward.

I went to my therapist for about five months, at which point I felt like I could move forward the rest of the way on my own. It wasn't the last time. Since then, I have had other bouts where I decided to go back to therapy to work through certain isolated situations. It was enlightening and helpful each time. If you have gone and found it wasn't for you, maybe try a different therapist. Sometimes, it takes a while to find a great fit. You don't have to commit to a lifetime of professional help, but try it and see what it does. It is not selfish or weak or anything negative. It is a brave power move.

In the 2019 novel *Evvie Drake Starts Over* by Linda Homes, the main character Evvie has gone through a traumatic loss and comes to the conclusion that she should try talking to a therapist. During her first session, she is feeling so silly about the whole thing, reflecting on the fact that she has so much to be grateful for: a support system, money in the bank, and her mental faculties about her, and she shouldn't *need* a therapist. She thinks she should just be able to figure this all out on her own. The response that her therapist gives is both unexpected and beautiful. She asks Evvie, *"Did you know it's possible to remove your own teeth with pliers?... If you have a bad tooth, you can take a pair of pliers, stick them in there, and pull as hard as you can."* She asks Evvie if that sounds like something she would do.

After thinking it might be a trick question, Evvie tells her no, she doesn't think she would do such a thing. The therapist responds by telling her that the whole analogy is similar to therapy and that one could always try to work things out by themselves. That idea is never in question. It might be more difficult, maybe even more dangerous, but you could still try. But just like there are alternatives to pulling out your own tooth with a pair of pliers, there are alternatives to trying to fix all of your mental and emotional wellness problems on your own. As we have explored throughout this book, we are not meant to navigate this grief alone. There are times in our lives when we will be the strong ones, the ones who are there for others and have it all pulled together. Sometimes, however, especially after a major loss, it is okay to admit that you are the one who needs support. Talking things out in the presence of an unbiased, skilled professional can be transformative. Please remember that seeking therapy is an act of self-compassion and courage. It allows you to hold space for the myriad of memories you are processing related to your loved one, but it also provides strategies and tools that will provide light in the dark, a new perspective, and greater hope.

PAUSE AND REFLECT:

If you have not yet made an appointment with a counselor, how do you imagine speaking to a counselor might help you with your grief? If you've already seen a counselor, how did it help you?

Sharing is Caring

Please
Keep sharing pictures of the kids on their first day of
school, your dogs on a walk, your afternoon spent at the
pumpkin patch, the Christmas tree all decorated. Share
about the band reunion tour that you scored tickets for,
on the floor. Keep going with the "We celebrated our
20th anniversary and here we are at our favorite hibachi
place. Here we are in Hawaii. Here we are at home in our
pajamas." Celebrate the love and that you made it this
far. Tell us that you're 365 days cigarette-free, 6 months
since you've touched a bottle, 10 years clean, training for
a marathon, training for a new job. Tell us how you've
seen the goodness of God reflected in a sunset, a win, a
dance in the rain. If it makes you come alive, tell the
world, because the world needs people who have come alive.

13

The Resistance to Isolation

"I'm over it, and it hasn't even begun. I don't even want to shop for presents," I told my sister at the start of our first holiday season after Mom died. I was not feeling the magic of the season; I did not want to wrap things up with ribbons and bows, and visions of sugarplums were not dancing in my head. I was eye-rolling at all of it, annoyed and saddened, and tired of dealing with all of these "firsts" without Mom. I thought Jenny might commiserate with me and join in on my bleakness. I mean, she was experiencing the same loss, so she must feel the same, right? Of course not, as I had forgotten the cardinal theme of grief: no two people's grief journeys are exactly the same. Her response was something to the effect of, "Well, sorry. We just can't have it that way. We can't fast forward and be done. There isn't a way *around* it. The only way is *through*." She went on to remind me, firmly but lovingly, that I had young children and that THEY had a mother who was still very much alive. They were not in the same doldrums of grief that I was. They still thought Christmas was beautiful and magical and truly the most wonderful time of the year. They didn't deserve to have to skip all of the fun stuff because I was having a hard time. I had to pull together my strength for them. So maybe I would feel like a turtle sludging her way through a mud pit, but somehow, for the sake of my kids, I would make it through.

You might be feeling like I was during that first holiday season: not wanting to be around anyone, not wanting to engage in anything, not wanting to deal with any potentially awkward social interactions—basically wanting to be a hermit. As we try to make sense of our loss, it seems easier to just be alone. After you lose a loved one, it is not uncommon to want to retreat, form a cocoon around yourself with a thick blanket, and hide away from the rest of the world. The grief can feel so overwhelming, and isolation might seem like the only plausible solution. If we are alone, we don't have to navigate anyone else's emotions, and we don't even have to confront our own. It seems like a win-win.

However, while alone time has its place in the healing process, *prolonged* isolation can make things worse in the long run. It can have detrimental effects on our well-being. In this chapter, we will explore a few reasons why staying isolated all the time after a loss is not advisable, as well as offer insight into the healing power of connection.

In the early stages of grief, when we are still full of shock and emotional overwhelm, some isolation can be needed and helpful. It is important to give yourself boundaries and not force yourself to be "okay" before you're ready. It's just as important to recognize that staying isolated for an extended period can negatively impact our mental, emotional, and even physical well-being. Consider the following possible negative impacts:

Deeper Grief: Isolating yourself can amplify your feelings of loneliness and despair. When we sequester ourselves from others, we miss out on the support, empathy, and shared experiences that can help ease our suffering. Grief then becomes a lonely, unrelenting burden that seems nearly impossible to bear.

Emotional Stagnation: Grief is not static but a dynamic process. It requires us to adapt to new realities, no matter that we never asked for them, and new emotions. Isolation can impede this adaptation, keeping us stuck in a cycle of negative thoughts and feelings. Interacting with others, even if it feels awkward at times, can help us process and evolve through our grief.

Lack of Perspective: When we stay isolated, it's easy to get trapped in our own echo chamber of thoughts and feelings. If we felt a little guilty before, that will be amplified. If we were angry before, it will only grow when we are by ourselves. Interacting with others, however, will give us new and fresh perspectives, greater self-empathy, new insights, and a deeper understanding of our grief and what we have gone through.

While we are aware that we should not stay in a prolonged state of isolation, we should also realize the important value of connection with others. Here are some key reasons why connection needs to be a part of our healing process:

Shared Grief: When we talk to and connect with others who have also experienced loss, we find comfort in that shared understanding. This might look like joining an online or in-person grief support group. It might look like talking to a friend or family member who has faced a similar loss. It helps to know we are not alone in our pain.

External Support: Friends, family, and other supportive groups can offer emotional support, a listening ear, and practical help in your time of grief. Remember the previous chapter on the helpers and how you don't want to prohibit them from being a blessing in your life? Let people share the load and carry the burden in practical ways instead of feeling like you have to do every single thing on your own.

Reclaiming Joy: Grief is heavy, deep, and a necessary part of the process after a loss, but it is not the entirety of our experience.

Grief and joy are not mutually exclusive. Connecting with others can lead us to moments of joy and laughter, both of which are important as we heal.

Both solitude and connection have their place in the healing process, and it is ideal to strike a balance between the two. Yes, there will be times to honor the need for solitude so you can be introspective and process your feelings. Please allow yourself this time without any guilt. It is necessary. But if the weight of isolation is too heavy, reach out to friends, family, a therapist, or a support group. Don't hesitate to ask for help or simply share how you are feeling with someone you trust. The healing power of connection and vulnerability cannot be overstated. Through sharing our grief, accepting support, and reclaiming our joy, we find internal strength and resilience when we most need it.

PAUSE AND REFLECT:

Do you tend to isolate for a prolonged period during difficult times? What is one small step you could take to encourage connection?

Lessons

He always let me
    Help in the garden
Every little bit
    Makes a difference,
Punkin' Seed, he would say

He taught me how
    To use his typewriter
Fingers on the home row
    It's okay to make mistakes
We have Wite-Out for that

She taught me how
    To look at the colors
Trees are more than green
    But blues and reds and browns
You just have to look closely

14

The Lessons Learned

On a summer day when I was about nine or ten years old, I was riding in the backseat of my Grandma Dixon's Oldsmobile, reading a chapter book, lost in the story, and I was jolted back to reality when she called my name. There was a line of trees up ahead—a mix of pines, maples, oaks—all looming in front of us as we drove south from the countryside of my hometown towards the Detroit suburbia of her house where I'd be staying for a few summer days.

"Do you see those trees, Christina? What color are those trees?" she asked. I felt like it must be a trick question, but I answered with the only logical answer, the one I'd known to be true since preschool. "They're green." I didn't say "duh," but I wondered where this could be going.

"Sure," she replied. "They are green, yes, but there's so much more to them. They are blue, red, brown, and yellow. They are so much more than just one thing." I know Grandma loved to paint. And so, I could reason; perhaps she was just thinking of the colors she would put on her palette were she to paint this scene later in her makeshift basement painting studio. She could have been looking at the trees from a creative standpoint. However, as

I grew, this statement always stuck with me, and I realize now that she likely meant more. I can see that in the way she heaped love on everyone, gave them grace after mistakes, forgave them, and encouraged everyone around her to see the good in people. She knew that people were also more than just one thing. It is easy to make snap judgments and use one word to describe a person, especially if you don't particularly like them. But like trees, it's not just one color or one word that defines a life; it's a mix of so many things. Sometimes, you just have to look closer to see. Grandma lived this out, too. Everyone was welcome in her home. I heard her speak ill of zero people in the eighteen years I was privileged enough to know and love her.

Grandma was trusting to a fault—literally—as she learned one time in downtown Detroit when she was trying to find the local jail in order to bail out a family member. She got a little lost and saw what she assumed was a nice young lady wearing a cropped top and a very short skirt on a street corner. *An angel!* She thought. *Someone who can help me!* So she rolled down the window, poked her head with pixie-cut gray hair out of it, and asked the "nice lady" if she could direct her to the local jail on such-and-such street. Well, what do you know, the nice lady would do more than tell her—she would show her!

So the lady got in the passenger seat under the pretense that she would tell Grandma how to get where she needed to go. But instead of telling her, she proceeded to take a pistol out of her small handbag and demand that my sweet, trusting, Italian grandmother give her her purse and all of her money. Grandma complied, the not-so-nice lady got out of the car, and Grandma sped away, understandably shaken and upset. She ended up finding her way back to the expressway and made it home, knowing that the family member she was about to bail out could use the overnight stay there anyway to do some serious thinking.

Everyone was grateful Grandma made it home safe that night, but it just goes to show how trusting (if a bit naive) she was. She understood that people were more nuanced than just black and white and contained multiple shades and layers, much like the trees we spotted on the side of the road, much like the mountains or sunsets she would paint in that makeshift basement studio, much like life in general. So many layers, so many colors, not just one thing or the other. Look closely.

Grandpa Conde was so proud of his garden. Grandma took care of the flower beds in front of the house and on the side of the house. But if you walked out the basement door, across the brick patio that Grandpa laid himself soon after they bought the house, and into the backyard, there was that 20x20 fenced-off space that was Grandpa's oasis. About half of it was a raspberry patch, with the rest being a mix of tomato plants, peppers, and various squashes. And whenever I came to visit, which was often, I was fascinated by everything he did in that garden, and I always wanted to help. He could have told me no or sent me inside to watch a cartoon on their boxy Zenith TV and Betamax video player. He could have told me to go inside and read so he could enjoy the quiet peace of his garden alone. But he never told me no; he never sent me away. He always let me help. When I felt like I didn't pull nearly as many weeds as he did (because I didn't) or that I didn't get them out by the roots as effectively as he did (because, again, I didn't), he would gently remind me, "It's okay, every little bit helps. It all adds up." I still think about this when I'm in my own garden, tackling my own big project, or having my kids help with household tasks. It all adds up. Every little bit helps.

There are microstories, too, little bits that remind me of what I have learned from all of my people. Grandpa also taught me to love books and to read voraciously, as he knew it would expand my worldview and perspective, that books could be my place of safety and also my window into what might be. Grandma Conde took me to the library when I was four years old. I was living with them temporarily, and she signed me up to get my very own library card. She sat me in a chair in her den beforehand and had me write my name over and over again. *Christina Pascarella, Christina Pascarella, Christina Pascarella*, which was a long name for a four-year-old, but she wanted to teach me so I could sign the back of the library card all by myself.

Grandma Conde also taught me to be unafraid in the kitchen, telling me if I could read a recipe, I could cook anything I wanted. She taught me that quality was more important than quantity in terms of material goods and almost everything else. My dad (although our relationship was limited because I was so young when he died, and our family dynamics were so tumultuous before that) still taught me many things, both directly and indirectly. I learned to appreciate oldies music from him and to dance in the kitchen, which is worth a thousand other smaller lessons.

And Mom. Oh, Mom. I learned that most people are just trying to do the best they can with the cards they have been dealt, and some people were dealt a really rough hand. So be kind. I learned that parenting is hard, the hardest job ever, but she did it with layers of trauma, mental illness, and shame—and while widowed. Be kind. I learned to love a variety of musical genres, including Broadway and movie musicals, again worth a million other smaller lessons. I learned that compassion is key to forgiveness and that McDonald's apple pies are delicious. I learned that mothers and daughters share a bond that is unexplainable. I learned that I raised her while she raised me and that there was beauty in the middle of all that frustration.

Saying goodbye to our loved ones is never easy. Their absence is painful, and we mourn for them. But while we say goodbye to their physical presence, we can welcome the way their presence and lessons continue to provide us with wisdom and influence. From them, we learn the importance of cherishing each moment, each memory, each raspberry, each oldies song. From them, we understand the significance of trust, nuance, empathy, and love. In this way, their lives can impact not just us but the next generation of our families and the generations to come after us. A single life and loss, as well as the lessons learned, do not just impact one person but create a ripple effect that lasts, for better or worse, for years to come. Our people may be gone, but the lessons they passed on to us will continue to live on, guiding us forward through the ups and downs of life.

PAUSE AND REFLECT:

What lessons will you carry with you from your loved one? What is a lesson learned from them that you want to be sure to teach someone else in your lifetime?

PART 3

HOPE

Last Wishes

If you were here
You'd want to see us
Smile, for while we are
Mourning, we are also
Living, giving the best
Of ourselves to this world
Growing, and knowing
It's okay to laugh in the middle
Of

    It

      All

15

The Laughter

I was just a kid when we said goodbye to my dad. The funeral home felt heavy with sorrow, but amidst it all, a buzz of people, family, and friends poured in to pay their respects. My father was one of nine siblings with an Italian mother who loved everyone and was loved in return. The visitation was full of people in and out all day. Someone had thought to bring coloring and activity books, which were a blessing, especially for us kids. Those books were packed with stickers, and we went to town, sticking them on everything—even our skirts! Can you imagine? Here we were, dressed in our darkest clothes, covered in rainbow animal stickers. It was like a little rebellion, a moment of joy in the midst of sadness.

I remember sneaking off to the bathroom, needing a breather from it all. Standing there, staring at my reflection, I couldn't help but give a broad-faced smile at the sight of me in my Goodwill skirt and those itchy tights, stickers adorning my outfit and my arms. But then, as I looked closer, that smile faded. Guilt washed over me like a wave. I was alone with my thoughts, just me and the mirror, facing up to the reality of why we were all there.

At only eight years old, I wasn't quite sure what was allowed. Dad was gone, so was I allowed to laugh? Have fun? Smile? Should I be in trouble for this? Should I feel guilty? And at that moment, I did. I felt like I should have been more downcast. I looked in the mirror and practiced frowning. I walked out of the bathroom with quiet resolve, thinking I should probably be more serious and sad, given the circumstances. Alas, I don't think it lasted long. My cousins were still there with sticker books and jokes and silly faces. I felt so conflicted. I wish I could tell my eight-year-old self that it's okay to laugh and smile. The tears will come; they have their place. But laughter is essential, too.

Everyone I know who has faced great tragedy and loss can re-tell some anecdote about something that happened in the middle of it that was so ridiculous or so juxtaposed against the sadness that it made them crack up. There's a common misconception that if you laugh or smile, you must not be sad or that you are being disrespectful to the loved one who has departed. But I disagree. Of course, there's a time and a place, which will differ depending on the circumstances. But when you think of your loved one and what they would want, chances are they wouldn't want you to be sad forever. They wouldn't want sorrow to overrule every other emotion for the rest of your life. You get one life to live. Live it well. Believe me, you will be plenty sad. Tears will fall by the bucketful. So, if something brings you joy in the middle of it all, lean in. According to numerous studies, laughter has many short and long-term health benefits and is proven to relieve tension in your body, increase endorphins, and, in the long run, improve your immune system, pain levels, and overall mood. Don't feel guilty for it.

When my mom was in hospice, and we knew she only had a few days left, my sister, Jenn, had the forethought to suggest that she and I go to the funeral home ahead of time to make some plans. We agreed that we should make decisions while we were somewhat clear-headed versus after the fact when we would be in full-on grief mode. This, by the way, is a highly recommended tip if you are ever given the choice.

We sat down with the funeral director and made the requisite choices, knowing that parts of it were easy and parts of it were hard. Many decades prior, my grandparents had bought two plots in a nearby cemetery, imagining they would be buried there someday. However, when tragedy struck and their only son, my Uncle Jeff, was killed in 1991, they buried him in one of the plots and left the other one for Mom. That part was taken care of at least, but we needed to decide how the funeral would go, how many viewing hours there would be, if there would be a luncheon afterward, what music would play, and what her obituary would say. So many choices. Then, the director led us to a room where all of the caskets were on display and left us to our own devices while she handled some work in her office. She said she would be back to check on us soon. Our brother couldn't be there in person, but we wanted to get his input on what style of casket to choose. So we FaceTimed him, and while Jenny held the phone and described the various options, I decided it would be a good idea to play Vanna White and pose by each one, waving my hands around to point out the highlighted features. We couldn't stop laughing at the ridiculousness of it all. I was feeling pretty grateful that I resisted the urge to climb in to give Tim and Jenny the full visual rendering since the funeral director had just walked in at that moment—Jenny and I were in a fit of giggles because she had just pointed to a black casket and told me pointedly, "When I go, make sure you put me in a black one." She looked me in the eyes and said with a deadpan expression, "What? Black makes me look skinny." This is after we had seen the urns, and Jenny reminded me that after her eventual viewing, she wants to be cremated and divided up between all of her children, with each container etched with the phrase, "Does this urn make my ash look big? Love, Mom." After the funeral director assured us it could have been weirder since she had been in this profession for several decades and had seen it all, she led us back into the office, where we finalized our decisions.

During that same horrible yet beautiful, depressing yet filled-with-gratitude week, Jenny and I were talking while sitting vigil at the nursing home, and she said, "You know what I just realized?"

"What's that?" I asked.

"Sometime in the very near future, we are going to see almost everyone who loves us, almost everyone who knew Mom, everyone who wants to pay their respects at the funeral," she explained.

"Gosh, that's right. It's going to be overwhelming, a little, don't you think?" I said.

"Well, yeah, but Kid (side note: being the older sister, she has called me Kid ever since I was little, and I know it will be my nickname from her no matter my age), I haven't had my hair done in almost two years. I can't see people like this." She grabbed her light brown mane, wide-eyed for effect. Naturally, since at that point we knew our mom's time was coming but not immediately imminent, I did what needed to be done: booked her a hair appointment and myself a nail appointment at my favorite local salon while my husband sat by Mom's bedside to be with her and to update us in the event anything changed. I fear as I type this that it all may seem trivial or vain, that some readers may clutch their pearls at the idea of leaving my mom's side, but as busy, working moms and daughters, Jenny and I were being practical. And going two years without a haircut for her and a manicure for me shows that vanity is not in our typical repertoire. At the salon, I selected my nail color, never veering from a classic red. And then came the small talk from the manicurist, who knew I was there with my sister, seemingly for a fun girl's day out, though our exhausted eyes might have shown otherwise.

"So, any special occasion?" she innocently asked.

I couldn't help it. The question struck me as so misplaced, so outlandish, and I'm sure the previously mentioned exhaustion had something to do with it, too, but I just started laughing.

"Well, um, actually, we're getting ready for a funeral," I replied.

The poor, sweet nail tech wasn't sure what to do with the juxtaposition of my laughter and my response. She stared for an extra beat, wondering what to say next, landing on, "Oh, I am so sorry. Who passed away?" as sensitively as she could. Bless her heart. But that just did me in even more because the proper answer was "no one." No one actually HAD died yet, even though Mom was certainly very close. We were just doing some preemptive funeral prepping, and the awkwardness of having to explain this to her made me want to laugh even more. As quickly as I could, I explained the situation, and from then on, we made small talk on safer topics, such as the weather and where she was in her apprenticeship trajectory. She could file this experience under "things I wasn't prepared for my client to say." Of course, after my nails were done and Jenny's hair was done, we got in the car, and I told her about my horribly awkward but hilarious conversation. We laughed about it together, again feeling like the lack of sleep might have something to do with our slap-happy responses under the circumstances.

Laughing is allowed. Smiling is allowed. For you, it may come right in the middle of the mess. For others, the laughter might not be something you find again until weeks or months after your loss. As with everything grief-related, there is no set timeline. But you don't have to feel guilty for finding joy or laughter in the middle of your grief. The two things are not mutually exclusive. The best way to honor those we have lost is to remember to live our best lives and live as fully as we can. Living fully includes any or all of the following: laughing, noticing the beauty of flowers in bloom, listening to the waves lap against the shore and allowing the sound to bring you peace, watching a comedy special, watching a sappy movie, going for a walk, or eating a piece of cake. In your grief, do not forget to live. On the one-year anniversary of Angie's death, I honored her and her punk rock persona by putting on a pair of Converse All-Stars (her favorite) and finding things that made me laugh. She was the funniest person I had ever met, with the quickest wit, best joke delivery, and sharpest comebacks. If I wanted to honor and remember her, I could do so best by seeking humor and laughing. Don't get me wrong, there are times to cry, sob, scream, and wail. Oh, Lord, are there ever. But when the opportunity presents itself where you feel you can smile again, laugh again, find joy again—DO IT.

If I could go back and tell eight-year-old me that it's okay to laugh, I would. Since I can't, I will tell you. Find joy again. Find laughter whenever you can. No matter if you are eight years old or eighty-eight years old, it is okay to let laughter in. You don't have to practice frowns in front of the mirror or feel guilty for experiencing a full range of emotions from happiness to sorrow. It is all a part of what makes us human.

PAUSE AND REFLECT:

Did you have any sort of reaction the first time you laughed or felt positive after your loved one passed?

After The Funeral

Walking through La Rosa Grocery Store
On Orchard Lake Road
He opens the glass door
To grab her a French Cruller
The plastic tongs pinching it,
suspended in midair
Held by his unsteady hands
And then—it hits him like a tidal wave

After 60 years,
She's not home anymore
To enjoy it.
Putting the pastry down,
And sliding the tongs back in their designated slot
He wipes his eyes,
turns back to the cart
And puts one foot in front of the other.

16

The Traditions, Old and New

Grandma Dixon was a hearty and loving Italian woman who came with her family to America when she was just a baby. She survived growing up during the Great Depression, getting married in the middle of World War II, having three children in quick succession, becoming a young widow, and then getting remarried and adding six more children to her family. With eleven mouths to feed, a working-class income, and her Italian roots running deep, homemade pasta was an important meal in the family. In fact, since they couldn't always afford roasts or hams, she created a family tradition of making homemade ravioli for the family to enjoy on Christmas Day—plus, what Italian family doesn't love pasta?

This tradition was passed on to her nine children, and as they married and had their own children, the family kept growing and growing, and the tradition evolved a bit. Instead of making the dough and the filling and piecing it all together on Christmas Eve to enjoy the following day, the family would gather together the Saturday after Thanksgiving to make all of the "ravs," as we called them. Grandma or the eldest aunts would mix the dough, and then Grandma would roll it out with the three-foot rolling pin given to her by her beloved first Italian mother-in-law, Great Grandma Pascarella. My sister has that rolling pin today, and she might protect it just as much as (if not more than) her four children. It's so special.

There were always other jobs to be done, also. You could mix the fillings—there was always meat as well as cheese-filled ravioli. Or you could be a "Spooner," who would put a small bit of filling on each square of pasta, or a folder, who would stretch the ends of the pasta over the filling to begin the process of closing it. Or the job that lent itself to the most mildly inappropriate jokes: the forker. A forker would press the tines of the fork onto the edges of the folded ravioli to seal it shut. It was an important job because if done poorly, it would cause all of the filling to seep out, and the ravs would essentially be ruined. However, once you got the hang of it, it was very easy, so it was a perfect job for all the young cousins. Plus, as tweens and teens, we enjoyed being allowed to say things like, "I'm doing the best forking job out of all of us!" and "This is so forking fun."

The tradition still takes place, but it is understandably different now that Grandma and the two eldest Pascarella sisters are gone. Other family members have moved to different states and aren't always able to come back for the holidays. It's the same, but not the same. It's continued but in a different way. We can't travel back in time as much as we wish we could. Instead, we are faced with a bit of a paradox: the need to hold on to traditions that connect us to the past while also allowing room for new ones that will carry us into the future. Traditions, both old and new, can give us a source of comfort and stability as we navigate our losses and remember the ones we have loved and lost.

Traditions can take shape in a million different ways. It could be an annual family reunion, a certain recipe made in the exact same way for the same occasion every year, or a weekly phone call to catch up. These rituals can be comforting, but they can really shake us up when things go off the rails and traditions change because a loved one passes. However, sometimes, these traditions can continue with the ones who are still around, and they allow us to keep the presence of our loved ones alive in our hearts and minds. The traditions we decide to continue demonstrate the legacies left by the ones we have lost. When we continue traditions, it ensures that the impact they left on our lives stays strong.

There are many examples of existing traditions that you could continue after their passing. Anniversaries and birthdays are undoubtedly difficult after a loss, but you can still use those days to celebrate a life lived or a love shared. Another example of an existing tradition could be a special shared meal, such as the ravioli my family still enjoys at Christmastime. Even though it feels different without Grandma there, it would likely feel worse if we abandoned the meal altogether. If your loved one cared about or volunteered with a certain charity or organization that meant a lot to them, continuing that practice can be a practical and beautiful way to keep their memory alive. Finally, visiting their favorite places and spending time in locations they loved can be a tradition you may want to keep. It might be their favorite local deli, or it might be an annual vacation in another country. It might just be sitting in their favorite spot on the back porch; it doesn't have to be elaborate to be meaningful.

As we navigate our grief journey, we must also be open to the idea of starting new traditions. Creating something new does not mean you are betraying your past but is simply a recognition of the need to adapt, overcome, and evolve after a loss. As we create new traditions, we acknowledge the change and the pain of our loss, but also the sense of renewal and healing that these new traditions can bring. When my mom was alive, I would typically bring her a treat of some kind on her birthday, visiting her with a small cake, cupcakes, apple pies from McDonald's, her favorite milkshake, or something similar. These days, that tradition is different and very bittersweet. Since she has passed, I visit her gravesite on her birthday, bringing a McDonald's apple pie with me, eating it while I sit on the ground and talk to her grave, giving her life updates like she's right there listening. Is she, really? No one can say for sure, but it makes me feel better and hurts no one, so I do it. New traditions can help us—not to forget but to keep moving forward.

New traditions can take shape in your life in many different ways. For example, you might begin a new self-care routine or ritual to help you cope with your stress and grief. Or you might consider starting the tradition of performing a particular act of kindness, making a donation, or doing something significant in your loved one's memory to keep their spirit alive. This may be less of a tradition per se and more of a project, but you might implement some sort of group project with your family or friends in the wake of a loss, like planting a memorial garden, establishing a scholarship like we did for Angie, or planning a benefit to honor the person you miss.

As we move forward, we must do our best to find a balance between holding on to old traditions and embracing new ones. Doing so will look different for everyone and is a deeply personal process. Be gentle with yourself as you go about this. Sometimes, it can feel like we are walking on a tightrope, with our past at one end and the future at the other. One misstep and we could fall—at least, that's what our mind tells us. But the truth is, there is no perfect right or wrong way to navigate this balance. Your journey is your own, and you have the flexibility to choose which traditions you cling to and which new ones to create. Don't be afraid to find comfort in the familiar and to forge new paths toward the new normal of the future, where your new traditions can serve as beacons of hope and healing. It is in the blend of old and new that we find greater resilience, relief, and comfort.

PAUSE AND REFLECT:

What traditions matter to you? What do you want to continue? What new tradition(s) might you want to adopt?

Just a Mirage

Missing you is like reaching for a piece of fruit in the wooden bowl
Except nothing is there

Missing you is like cozying up with a blanket, but then realizing,
The covering is inexplicably gone

Missing you is like walking through the desert and spotting water
Finally, only to realize it was
Just a mirage

17

The Life to Live

A few months after my mother died, my husband and I had about 60 hours of childcare secured for our three young children right around the time of our twelfth wedding anniversary. This was a miracle, as we often struggled to coordinate a sitter just for one evening out, let alone a multi-day period. I started crowdsourcing recommendations for where to go, posting on social media asking for suggestions for the best spot in Michigan for a weekend getaway with no kids. I was met with dozens of helpful responses, many of which suggested popular northern Michigan hot spots. However, one comment in particular stuck out to me. My older sister, who would be the one watching the kids for the weekend, suggested this:

"I vote you get out of Michigan. Find a cheap flight somewhere, and don't look back—except to get your kids. Please come back for them."

I sat on that idea for a few hours, letting it ruminate in my mind. I began thinking, realizing that the time it would take us to drive to many of the suggested Michigan spots would be roughly the same time it would take to fly to a farther destination. Like all the best plans, it started with a few questions. Namely: what if?

And why not? What if we went to a spot that had always been on my dream list of places to visit? What if we just booked the tickets and went? Why not go big, if only for a short weekend?

So we booked tickets, got a tiny hotel room with a view of the Empire State Building, and went to New York City. It was only a few months after losing Mom. I was still clearing the fog of grief. Traveling helped, especially going to as large of a melting pot as New York. Seeing so many other people in one giant city, remembering we are all taking it day by day and all have a story to tell and a life to live—that helped, too. Being in the middle of such a huge city with so many others from all walks of life allowed me to experience a shared connection with the rest of humanity. It allowed me to think deeply about my own life and what I wanted to do with it.

Many days in that season, the post-losing-Mom season, I was still untangling the messy knot of emotions that I inherited with her passing. Grief was and is such an arduous process. But one thing I learned while working through all of it, for which I am most grateful, is that I want to spend my life living.

My mom had 68 years.

My dad had 48.

Angie had just shy of 28.

You never know what is going to happen or when. Every day, every year, every moment is such a gift. For as long as I could remember, I had wanted to visit New York City. That early summer weekend, celebrating my wedding anniversary as well as life itself, I did it. It was a whirlwind and one of the best trips I could have ever imagined. The city was everything I thought it would be and more. It was loud and wonderful, tiring and energizing all at once. It was a wonderful trip, and I am glad I asked the "what if" and "why not" questions. It was energizing to do a big (to me) thing and take a leap. My challenge to you, my friends, is to do the thing. Do the thing you say you want to do but haven't done yet. It can be a big thing or a small thing, but do it. Visit the place you want to visit but haven't made time for. Do the thing that scares you.

Book the ticket.

Plan the girls' night.

Write the screenplay.

Run the race.

Get the degree.

Make amends with the person.

Ride the roller coaster.

Audition for the part.

Live the life.

Live it while you still can. Our time is so precious and so limited in the grand scheme of things. If losing our loved ones teaches us anything, it is that time is short, and you never know what might happen, so use the time wisely while you still can. Death forces us to consider our own mortality, that's for sure. Going back to the earlier idea of the List of 100 Dreams, don't forget to cultivate the life you want and live with intentionality. It doesn't mean you have to be in constant striving or overachieving mode, but rather, it is an invitation to go after what matters to you and fill your life with beauty and joy. Life is too short to be filled with anything less. It's also important to note that (if I were a betting woman, I would be willing to bet) there is a lot of beauty and joy around you already, so be sure to notice it in the midst of the hard. The wag of a dog's tail, the way flowers bloom in the spring, the changing colors of leaves in autumn, the perfectly timed joke in your favorite TV show, the "yes" or the "no" that you needed to hear at the right time, the smell of coffee in the morning or the slow-burning candle on your kitchen counter at night... count it all as the beauty that it is. Recognize it. Appreciate it. Embrace it.

Be gentle with yourself as you grieve, but also be open to opportunities for growth and experiences that bring joy. It's okay to smile, to laugh, and to embrace life even amid the pain of loss. Cling tight to the memories of your loved ones while also acknowledging that life continues and it's up to us to make the most of it.

Remember, just like my spontaneous trip to New York City, sometimes the best decisions are the ones made on a whim. Let yourself be guided by curiosity, the desire for adventure, and the urge to make the most of every day. Embrace the grief journey, knowing that it comes with its high highs and crashing lows, but in the midst of it all, you can still find moments of beauty, hope, and growth.

My mom liked playing the classic dice game Yahtzee. Once, when I was about 19 or 20 years old, I came back home for a visit from college. We played a few rounds of the game, and I somehow beat her every time. I didn't think too much about it when I went back to my dorm room a few days later.

A few months went by, and I went back for another visit, and I was driving Mom somewhere. A few things to note—at this time, our relationship was incredibly rocky, and it was rare for us to create positive memories together. In fact, driving around, we were arguing about something or other. Maybe I was lacking compassion, or she was being critical. Whatever it might have been, I remember there was tension. She was also living alone at the time, as I was off at college, and I know she was having a hard time and feeling lonely a lot. Meanwhile, I was working as a waitress while attending college and had just gotten engaged to my high school sweetheart. Wedding plans were on the horizon.

Life was busy. Anyways, we were driving and it started raining hard, drops pounding on my windshield as I drove on the highway. Someone sped past recklessly and cut us off to get ahead. I yelled out to the nameless driver, "Slow down! I'd like to make it home in one piece today!"

Mom added, "Yeah! We've got a lot to live for, you know." It was just an off-the-cuff remark, but I immediately thought of my engagement, my college degree, and the big expanse of life that was on the horizon. I was lost in thought when I heard Mom's voice again. She looked over at me and said, "I still need to beat you in Yahtzee."

At the time I thought, this is one of those moments and statements that I will remember forever, even though I wasn't sure why. Now, I understand that in my naive immaturity, I thought it was a silly thing for her to say. I felt a little sad for her. Here I was, looking forward to all of these big epic moments, and she just wanted to beat me in a dice game. Now, I get it. She just wanted time. Connection. Positive memories with a daughter with whom she struggled to connect, which is a big thing in and of itself. I know that now.

Maybe you have big plans on the horizon. Maybe not. Maybe your loss upended everything, and you don't know what lies ahead. Maybe you've accomplished everything you set out to do, and you just want to take things slow and seek connection with the ones you love. Maybe you want to visit every continent on Earth. Everyone is different. Life is a whirlwind, but it's *our* whirlwind. Embrace it, experience it, and live it while we still can. Let the memories of those we have lost inspire us to cherish the moments big and small and make the most of this precious gift called life. We have living left to do, and by doing so, we honor the loved ones we have lost, whether it is through something grand or by teaching our kids how to play Yahtzee.

PAUSE AND REFLECT:

What thing, seemingly big or seemingly small, do you want to do with this one precious life of yours? What is one step you could take towards making it happen?

Thought of You

"I thought of you today."
my middle schooler said at the dinner table,
unaware of the positive impact of his words.
Apparently he thought of me
when he saw a certain object
at cross country practice and it reminded him
of an inside joke we have.
He made a connection,
which led to a memory,
which led to a smile.

It reminded me that sometimes
we may never know the far-reaching impact
of our experiences and connections with others.
Sometimes they let us know.
Sometimes it never gets shared.
Maybe that kindness you extended
to a cashier gave her hope that
maybe humanity wasn't so vile after all.
Maybe a student believed in himself
because you did first.
Maybe that conversation you had with a friend
pulled them off of a ledge
you didn't even know they were standing on.

And then there are the "I thought of you"
moments that you would share,
but you can't because the person
is no longer here on earth.
Like how I think of my grandpa
and his garden every single time I eat a raspberry.
I think of my dad whenever I hear
Van Morrison's "Brown Eyed Girl."
I think of my mom when I see
Jack Daniels Salmon on the menu at E.G. Nicks.

I thought of you.
I thought of you.
I thought of you.

There's that quote that says
Nobody can do everything
but everybody can do something.
In terms of making the world a better place,
maybe something everybody can do is tell people,
"I thought of you" more often, and
see
what
happens

18

The Gratitude

During the darkest moments of grief, it might seem impossible to find anything to be grateful for. The pain of losing a loved one can overtake and consume us, leaving little room for anything else. This chapter does not in any way intend to minimize the hurt we feel in those moments. Yet amidst the sorrow, there are times when gratitude shines through unexpectedly, like a burst of light on a cloudy and stormy day.

I remember one moment during my own grief journey. It was a late November day, about eight months after Mom passed. It was my first holiday season without her, and I felt the weight heavy on my chest like a dropped barbell. We were putting up our Christmas tree, as we always do as a family, and I was feeling lost in my thoughts. Then, the Pandora Christmas radio station began to play Bing Crosby's classic "White Christmas," and the weight became unbearable. I could feel the tears instantly welling up in my eyes. My oldest son, who was about ten years old at the time and unsure how to comfort or react when surrounded by a big emotion, just whispered to my husband, "Um, Dad? Mom is crying again."

As I let the tears fall (remember, honoring our emotions is a good thing), I decided to keep going with the task at hand. I was honest with myself and my children: "Yes, sweetie, I'm crying because this song was Grandma Cam's favorite Christmas song, and I just miss her. It's normal to miss people when they are gone, especially during the holidays." I looked down in our ornament box to grab the next bulb. In the middle of my sadness and falling tears, I had to smile. It was an ornament that had once belonged to my grandma and grandpa, a beautiful red mid-century bulb with "Merry Christmas & Happy New Year" emblazoned on it amid sprigs of holly. I was thankful I had that and a few other precious mementos that reminded me of my grandparents and my mom. In that moment, I felt a glimmer of gratitude for the legacy I was a part of. It was a reminder that even in the middle of sorrow, there are always those moments of beauty, hope, and wonder. It was a reminder that gratitude has the power to heal, even during the most challenging times.

When we are grieving, it is natural to focus on what we have lost. We mourn the absence of the person we love and long for the days when they were here. So often, it just doesn't seem fair. It doesn't seem fair because it *isn't* fair. It might not seem okay because it's *not* okay. It's not okay that Dad didn't get to see me get married or meet his grandchildren. It's not okay that my grandpa didn't get to see me write my first book, or that I can't call Grandma to ask a question about a treasured recipe, or that Angie will always be 27, or that Mom won't ever call me again. None of those things are okay, and they never will be. That must be acknowledged.

And yet, even though those shadows of "this is not okay" will always hang over us, they will not always be so looming and prominent. They will not be so all-consuming forever and ever. The shadows will recede in different ways, and at different times, we are able to go on to create happy memories, have healthy relationships, and lead fulfilling lives. As we navigate through the grieving process and work towards that health and hope, embracing a mindset of gratitude can be a transformative and healing practice. Gratitude does not negate the pain of loss; instead, it allows us to find moments of solace and strength. When we can connect to things we are grateful for, it's like a beacon of light from a lighthouse, guiding a lost ship back to the shore, reminding us that even in our grief, there are always reasons to be thankful.

One of the beautiful aspects of gratitude is that it can be found in the simplest of things. It doesn't have anything to do with grand gestures or extravagant lifestyles; it's about finding joy in the everyday moments. It could be the warmth of a hug, the sound of laughter or your favorite song, or the feeling of the sun on your face during a walk outside. Every day that we are alive brings us much to be grateful for. We have to make a conscious choice to focus on that versus the negative or little inconveniences of life.

Gratitude is not about denying the pain but acknowledging the beauty that coexists with grief. It's about honoring the memories of our loved ones while also remembering they were whole, imperfect humans with their own quirks. Gratitude reminds us that we were blessed to have known and loved them.

How exactly can gratitude help you heal? Here are some powerful ways:

- **Shifting Perspective:** Gratitude shifts our focus from what we have lost to what we have, period. Instead of dwelling on the emptiness left by our loved one's absence, we begin to appreciate the fullness of the love and experiences we shared with them.
- **Finding Meaning:** Gratitude can help us find meaning in our grief journey. It allows us to see the lessons and blessings that can come from even the most painful experienc-

es. Through our gratitude, we can find a deeper sense of purpose and understanding.

- **Cultivating Resilience:** Grief can be overwhelming, and its intensity can make it easy to feel defeated. Gratitude acts as a source of resilience, giving us the strength to keep moving forward despite the pain.
- **Nurturing Connection:** Expressing gratitude fosters a sense of connection with others. Sharing our appreciation for those who support us during our grief journey strengthens our bonds and creates a supportive network of love and understanding. It also connects us to those we have lost, being grateful for the time we had with them and the memories we created, even if our hearts might always ache for more time.
- **Embracing Hope:** Gratitude ignites hope even in the darkest times. It reminds us that there is still goodness in the world and that life holds the potential for happiness and joy—even after, or maybe especially after, a loss.

In the middle of all of this, practicing gratitude doesn't mean we ignore the pain or pretend everything is okay because we all know it's not. It's okay to grieve, to cry, and to feel all of the emotions that accompany the loss. Think of gratitude as a companion that walks alongside grief, offering comfort, light, and hope in the middle of the cloud cover.

If you are struggling to find gratitude in the grieving process, know that it's okay to start small. Take a moment each day to pause and reflect on the things you are grateful for, even if they seem insignificant. Embrace the little sparks of joy that come your way because sparks can turn into bigger flames. Remember, it's not a destination but a continuous journey, a practice that evolves with time, just like grief itself. Some days, it will be easy to find things to be grateful for, while other days, it will feel like a monumental challenge. And that's okay.

Just like with all the other steps in the process, be patient and gentle with yourself as you explore the path of gratitude. Allow it to unfold naturally, and don't force yourself to feel a certain way. The power lies in authenticity, being able to genuinely appreciate the good things we encounter along the way. In the end, as you embrace the power of gratitude, you will find that healing is not at all about forgetting or moving on—as we already discussed, that doesn't happen—but rather moving forward, carrying the memory of your loved ones in your heart while also cherishing the beauty of the world around you. It's a gift to yourself and the person or people you have lost as you continue to live a full life of love in their honor.

PAUSE AND REFLECT:

What are some things for which you feel grateful right now?

Starry Eyed

It was one of those perfect summer nights
where the sun is still kissing everyone
Even as it sets, and the bugs are somewhere else,
Not touching you one bit.

I'm pulling a few weeds and doing a lotta nothing really
While the kids ride bikes in the driveway
The stars are coming over to hang out
And Jackson stops pedaling to look up

Hey mommy? A question is coming and it's gonna be deep.
So, is each of the stars, like, a person in heaven
Looking down on us?
Like they can see us but our eyes aren't strong enough to see them?

I go the pragmatic route and we talk about
The solar system and gasses and balls of light.
But wouldn't it be something if he were right?
If all the ones we loved and lost could stay in touch?

It's getting pretty dark now, so we walk inside.
I pass the picture of Mom hanging on the wall
I drink from a glass that I took from Grandpa's cabin before we sold it.
I look in the mirror. Those are Dad's eyes staring back at me.

Maybe it's not that they can see us.

Maybe each ball of light isn't their visage shining to us all the way from heaven.

But there are still other signs, other connections

Maybe we can still stay in touch after all.

19

The Connection to Creation

When I was a 4th-grade classroom teacher, my favorite week each year was the stretch where my class and I would take a bus each day for five days out to a local nature center and immerse ourselves in exploration, hiking trails, journaling at the side of a pond, and listening, looking, and appreciating what we heard and saw.

We spent hours outside, no matter the weather, integrating math, literacy, science, and survival skills into our daily lessons. The first year we did this, the week that my class was scheduled to go was the last week in the calendar rotation, so I thought it would be warmer with it being that much closer to spring. Ha! I was wrong. Our week ended up being the coldest, with temperatures hovering right around 12°. We are used to cold weather in Michigan, but this was extreme, even for us. Still, we had front-loaded with many lessons and notes home about appropriate clothing and gear.

We were more or less prepared, and the week ended up being amazing. Some of the very best parts of it were the nature journaling sessions. Each day, we would layer up with all of our warm gear, hike into the middle of one of the trails, and then find a spot to sit and journal. Each day, there was a focus question for each student, but they could expand on it or draw or write about what they saw, heard, smelled, or could touch. I encouraged the students to really be in tune with their senses and immerse themselves in the beauty of nature. At the end of the week, many of them reported that the journaling experience was their favorite part, too. Many of them had never before spent an hour at a time outside, just observing in silence. The outdoors can provide such a sense of calm—a sense of peace. It can lead us to a peace we didn't know existed.

Regardless of your faith background, being outside in the right environment can be a profoundly spiritual experience. Standing barefoot on a sandy beach with a lake or ocean stretching out in front of you, climbing a mountain, hiking in a forest, looking out at the indescribable vastness of the Grand Canyon—they all connect us to the Earth, and, in turn, to the Creator of it all. In times of grief and sorrow, I have found that spending time in nature gives me a renewed appreciation for God as an artist. The colors in the trees, the intertwining of roots, the markings on the birds—it's all incredible, intricate, complex, and beautiful, created by a loving God. And look at us with our incredible, intricate, complex, and beautiful thoughts, emotions, and lived experiences. We are all connected through creation, and we all matter to Him. There is great comfort in that.

A Bible passage that has been a balm to my soul many times over the years is Matthew 6:25-27:

"Therefore I tell you, do not worry about your life, what you will eat or drink; or about your body, what you will wear. Is not life more than food, and the body more than clothes? Look at the birds of the air; they do not sow or reap or store away in barns, and yet your heavenly Father feeds them. Are you not much more valuable than they? Can any one of you by worrying add a single hour to your life?"

These words have reminded me time and time again that worry is not my antidote to pain, sorrow, anxiousness, or any trouble I may be having. Of course, we are human, and worrying is a natural response in many situations, but that doesn't mean it should be our default or that it helps us. Let these words remind you that you are valued, cared for, and loved. That God loves you more than the birds in the sky or the flowers that grow in the fields, and yet there are provisions that ensure the growth of said birds and flowers. God will provide comfort, sustenance, and hope to ensure your growth as well. The birds, the trees, their roots, the sunlight, our beating hearts—we are all connected and part of this big, beautiful creation. Getting outside emphasizes this. Here are some ideas if you need a nudge:

Go barefoot if you can.
Drink your morning coffee on the porch.
Hike in the snow.
Hike in the summer.
Walk on a trail.
Walk in your subdivision.
Go to a local park.
Go to a National Park (There's a reason why Zion National Park is called Zion. Zion is a specific, historically significant location—the name refers to both a hill in the city of Jerusalem and to the city itself—but it's also used in a general way to mean "holy place" or "kingdom of heaven." It is the most awe-inspiring location I have ever personally seen. Visiting there for the first time, my jaw dropped and I am still telling everyone who will listen how amazing it is and that it should be on their bucket list.)
Walk along the beach.
Jump in the water.
Tube down a river.

Climb a mountain.
Eat a meal outside.
Look at the stars.
Nature photography.
Nature scavenger hunts.
Sit and observe outside.
Journal what you see.
Watch birds.
Walk a dog.
Dance in the rain.

During another school trip to the same nature center in early March 2018, I got a call from the nursing home about Mom. She was supposed to have surgery at the end of that week that would remove the cancer and give her another shot. Instead, the conversation with the charge nurse included the words "hospice" and "death process." I was floored. What? Death? Dying? She was supposed to have a chance! She was supposed to get the surgery. But no, the cancer was too vicious, too quick, and had caused a host of problems that were just too much for her body to handle. She was shutting down. I had no car at the nature center. I had to finish the afternoon with my students. Thankfully, we only had another hour to go. My mind was reeling, disconnected—like I was there but not really there.

Finishing up the last hike through the woods, I looked at the trees around me, somehow noticing the differences. Some of them were so tall and strong and confident in their roots—sturdy. Others were uprooted and falling over and looked like a jumbled mess. I remembered what the nature center guide told us earlier that week. She said that the trees in the forest that fall still serve an important purpose. The fallen trees can open up the woodland canopy and make room for more light to shine down. They provide a home for small animals and insects. And as the fallen trees decompose, they fertilize the ground, creating life—creating beauty from their breakdown.

I knew I was in a moment of emotional breakdown that day, just as my mom's body was beginning its earthly breakdown. I had no words to describe the shock, the sadness, the uncertainty I felt. I hoped and prayed that someday, somehow, beauty could be found in this story. It happened. The loss led to pain, yes, but it also led to a deeper appreciation for my mother, my roots, for my siblings, for my childhood (even the traumatic parts), my friends, my faith, and for my life in general.

You may feel so uprooted right now, a jumbled mess on the forest canopy floor, but this is not where your story ends. This is not all there is. This uprooting will lead to light; it will lead to new growth, new life, and hope. It might feel like only decay and sorrow, but that is not how it ends. There is more to your story. You are connected to the beauty of creation, connected to a Creator, and loved. May nature's presence in your life serve as a reminder that even in moments of profound loss and sadness, life continues its cyclical rhythms. Life, death, legacy, hope. Life, death, legacy, hope. Repeat.

PAUSE AND REFLECT:

What are some ways in which you enjoy spending time in nature?

Special Occasions

I inherited Grandma Conde's good china
The set they received for their wedding in 1942
With pink florals lining the edges
So delicate and beautiful, it merits marvel

At first I saved it for special occasions
Evelyn's tenth birthday party
The day the Queen of England died
And we taught ourselves how to make scones
In her honor

But being alive is a special occasion
Waking up to a new day is a special occasion
A random Wednesday is a special occasion
Let's use the good china
Whenever
    the
        mood
            strikes

20

The Purpose After Pain

A year after my mom died, a coworker of mine lost her own mother. My colleague was navigating her early 20s and would now journey through the rest of adulthood without her mom, who passed after a long fight against cancer.

Her mother died right before the last week of school. I assumed she would take leave for the remainder of the school year. Therefore, I was a little surprised to see my coworker standing at her classroom door, greeting her students with her trademark enthusiasm and warmth on the last day of school. She did not want to leave the last day celebrating to a substitute, and she felt that being around her students—she loves them so much, year after year—would be a balm to her soul. But still, she was fragile that day, telling people she didn't want hugs or to talk about "it," and of course, we all knew what "it" was. I had planned on mailing her a card, thinking I wouldn't see her at school, but realizing she was there that day, I took a different route. I jetted out to the store on my lunch break and looked in the sympathy card section. I hate that section. Nothing ever seems quite right. Those well-intentioned platitudes are not what we want to hear in the midst of our pain and suffering. What I wanted to tell her wasn't on a card. So I said, "Forget it. I'll make my own card." I took one that had a few words and maybe some flowers on the front and a few more boring words on the inside. I crossed off all the words and just wrote, "THIS SUCKS AND I'M SORRY. Love, Christina." Because really, that's all there was to say.

And it's the truth. It sucks to lose your mom. It sucks to lose a grandparent, a friend, a sibling, a child, a spouse—anyone you love. It's rotten and terrible and horrific, and all of the other words that mean hard and bad. Sometimes, there are just no deep and profound words that can describe the pain, and you don't want anyone to tell you that it's all going to be okay. Let me be angry! Let me just be upset about this! I just lost someone I loved! IT SUCKS, and that's all I need to say at the moment. And that's okay.

This is your permission to feel that in the moment. But that moment? It won't last forever. It won't last forever because you are committed to growth, healing, and honoring your loved ones by living full and free. You, reading this book right now, know there's more to mourning than just the sad parts. You know there is sad mourning, and there is good mourning, dark and light, lows, and highs. You know that beauty can be born from the ashes. You, as you heal, will use your story to help others. As renowned professor, author, and shame and vulnerability researcher Brené Brown says, "One day, you will tell your story of how you've overcome what you're going through now, and it will become part of someone else's survival guide."

My hand-scrawled words and my sympathy card to my friend were undoubtedly authentic, especially in light of the fact that I had gone through the very same thing. I was able to use my own experiences and think: what did I really need to hear in those early days of fresh grief? Did I need someone to tell me everything was going to be okay and that I should be grateful she was in a better place? NO! I needed someone to acknowledge how difficult and painful this was. How much it sucked. My pain points provided a purpose in that moment: to connect to my friend and help her feel better, even if marginally.

The same holds true for you. Someday, and maybe that day has already come for you, the story of what you have gone through, the struggles you have overcome, the mountains you have climbed, all of it can be used to help other people who are going through the same thing. Here's the thing: when we celebrate, we don't do it in isolation, right? When we win an award, there's usually some sort of ceremony and clapping. When a football team wins the Super Bowl, there is confetti and everyone who loves the winning team is whooping and hollering and jumping for joy. The coach gets a bucket of Gatorade poured on his head for Lord knows what reason, and everyone is sharing in the joy. We don't celebrate alone. Similarly, we are not meant to grieve alone, either. We are meant to grieve together, mourn together, hold space in our hearts for the sadness of others. So you, as one who has felt that profound sadness of loss, will someday be able to use that experience to help someone else as they go through something similar.

Remember, too, that this work is just as profound if you do it for only one person. What you do for one person matters just as much as what you could do for a thousand people. It all matters, so don't believe any lie that says it doesn't. The fact of the matter is that pain is a part of our story. Heaven help the person who thinks they will never suffer because the human condition isn't quite that smooth. There will be hurts, losses, and trauma of varying degrees for all of us. But it doesn't have to stop there. A bad thing happened to me. I lost a loved one. Is that the end? Nope, not the end. The end of one part of the story, yes. But not the end of the whole book. You keep going. You can't keep all of your feelings and traumas locked in the proverbial cage. Let them out. Embrace your vulnerability and, in turn, embrace your ability to help others. You can use the pain and what you have been through to provide a beacon of hope for someone else who will someday go through the same thing. You have the opportunity to use your story to change someone else's story, to change a life, to change your life, to *not* let your life become completely consumed by this bad thing that happened to you.

Are you going to use that opportunity? We both know the answer. Yes. You can do it.

I'M SO PROUD OF YOU.

PAUSE AND REFLECT:

What's next for you?

Acknowledgements

Where to begin? There are so many people who have helped me see this book across the finish line. Thank you to the team at hope*books. Your guidance, professional advice, community, and encouragement were invaluable.

I can't write a book about healing from losses without first having experienced losses in the first place. I would give anything for another day with you all. One more meal, one more joke, one more conversation, but alas, that's not the reality. I am grateful for the time that we did have and everything I learned, good and bad.

Dad, thank you for teaching me to appreciate good music and not be afraid to sing along.

Grandma Conde, thank you for teaching me the value of "please" and "thank you", teaching me how to cook, and that traditions are important.

Grandpa, thank you for nurturing my love of reading and writing, and teaching me to find silver linings in difficult situations.

Grandma Dixon, thank you for teaching me to look for the best in people, to show grace, and to look for all the colors.

Angie, thank you for the jokes and the laughter and the ridiculous shenanigans.

Mom, thank you for teaching me, in your own way, to look deeper than the surface, and about the power of forgiveness.

I miss you all so much.

Thank you to Amber, for the phone calls, texts, the "you can do this" reminders, and for believing in this project wholeheartedly.

To Jenny, Mary, and many other friends and family who checked in, asked for updates, sent encouragement--that meant the world and I appreciate you so much.

Chris, your support and encouragement gave me the kick in the pants that I needed to get this book written. And even though I didn't always want to hear it, your "Five minutes a day goes a long way" advice was sound and correct. Thank you for giving me space to write and for always making me think that I could do this and it wasn't a crazy idea.

To my children, I love you so much. Even though I'm a writer, I don't know that I could ever fully describe just how much I love you and how proud I am to be your mom. Thank you for being patient and understanding when I needed to write or when dinner was pizza, again (ha, like you would ever complain about that). You are the best.

And to you, my readers. Thank you for picking up this book. I pray that it helps you see the light in the dark.

Endnotes

Chapter Two
Sheeran, E. (2017). *Castle on the Hill*. On ÷ [Album]. Atlantic Records.

Chapter Four
Gold, A. (1978). *Thank You for Being a Friend*. On *All This and Heaven Too* [Album]. Asylum Records.

Chapter Six
Bridge, Andrew. *Hope's Boy: A Memoir*. Hachette Books, 2008.
Vanderkam, Laura. *I Know How She Does It: How Successful Women Make the Most of Their Time*. Penguin Books, 2015.
Godzilla: King of the Monsters. Directed by Michael Dougherty, performances by Kyle Chandler, Vera Farmiga, and Millie Bobby Brown, Warner Bros. Pictures, 2019.

Chapter Eight
Beaches. Directed by Garry Marshall, performances by Bette Midler and Barbara Hershey, Touchstone Pictures, 1988.

Chapter Nine
Ace of Base. "The Sign." *Happy Nation*, Arista Records, 1993.

Chapter Ten
Goodale's Bakery 500 Norway St,Grayling, MI 49738
Inside Out. Directed by Pete Docter, performances by Amy Poehler, Phyllis Smith, and Bill Hader, Pixar Animation Studios, 2015.

Chapter Eleven
https://advokatefoundation.com/

Chapter Twelve

Rocky Balboa. *Rocky*, directed by John G. Avildsen, United Artists, 1976.

Holmes, Linda. *Evvie Drake Starts Over*. Ballantine Books, 2019.

Chapter Fifteen

Wheel of Fortune. Hosted by Pat Sajak and Vanna White, NBC, 1983–present.

Chapter Seventeen

Yahtzee. Designed by Milton Bradley, Hasbro, 1956.

Chapter Eighteen

Crosby, Bing. "White Christmas." *Holiday Inn*, Decca Records, 1942.

Chapter Twenty

Brown, Brené. *Rising Strong: The Reckoning, the Rumble, the Revolution*. Spiegel & Grau, 2015.

Printed in the USA
CPSIA information can be obtained
at www.ICGtesting.com
CBHW031730191024
16012CB00001B/1